TONY LEONARD was born in the Fenland six miles from Ely. Now he's retired, happily and lives in Saint Ives near Huntingdon in C

After morning coffee, Tony enjoys playing classical music on his piano. Later on, in the afternoon, he's either busy writing plays or poetry. He sometimes performs his verse in the local Corn Exchange or the Dolphin Hotel.

The early evenings are reserved for listening to his CD collection. His musical tastes are varied from the swinging sixties to the present day and just about anything else between – anything that moves him.

Tony has an insatiable curiosity, a tendency to be obsessive and loves bringing historical myths and legends to life through his poetry, piercing the realms of time and relating to the thoughts of his distant ancestors.

Present-day celebrity culture never fails to fascinate Tony. Its fleeting nature has inspired some of the poems in this book.

He's also humorous, mischievous – a bit of a Jekyll and Hyde – and won't shy away from a debate, particularly politics and religion. He firmly believes in poetry as a medium to provoke discussions on controversial topics, sparking conversations that will hold the key to the future of the world we live in, for good or ill.

OUR
AMAZING
ENGLISH
HERITAGE

Poems exploring the influences
behind our British culture

Tony Leonard

SilverWood

Published in 2021 by SilverWood Books

SilverWood Books Ltd
14 Small Street, Bristol, BS1 1DE, United Kingdom
www.silverwoodbooks.co.uk

ISBN 9798566329321 (KDP paperback)

British Library Cataloguing in Publication Data
A CIP catalogue record for this book is available from the British Library

Page design and typesetting by SilverWood Books

To my wife Joy

Praise for Our Amazing English Heritage

"It has been a pleasure to be associated for the past decade with the quality and authenticity of Tony Leonard's Poetry. His writings are infused with the very essence of his 'Soham' heart and soul. His books are a joy to own and re-read over and again."

Chris Morgan

"Tony's work reveals the depth and passion he has for literature as a medium which is not only to be read but spoken aloud. Indeed, one could say it is when his verse and prose are spoken or performed that the real force of his work can be felt. It is epic in scale, historical often, encompassing myths and legends, the magical and the spiritual. It is stirring, atmospheric, raging at times, but always deeply felt and passionately presented. The intensity, attention to detail, the richness in the use of imagery and the all-consuming nature of the work is to be admired."

Collette Parker,
M.A. Cantab

Contents

Acknowledgements

I've dedicated this book to my wife Joy for all her love and support during my struggles. I've really appreciated her kindness, patience and sympathy particularly when the muse strikes me like lightning in the middle of the night.

I also dedicate this book to the many people who've influenced me over the years. The first person to spring to mind was during my childhood, Dora Ross divorced from a Scottish aristocrat, she was my music teacher and passionate about poetry. During my working life I met a Cambridge University lecturer, this young woman introduced me to a book that opened up the Anglo-Saxon world with its history and language. As the years rolled on, I attended a writers' group at a public school in Bury Saint Edmunds with a Scottish friend, hence the Celtic influence. Finally, in my later years a fellow poet, Chris Morgan, introduced me to performance poetry, where I performed my work for the first time at different local venues. I lapped up this wealth of experience listening to a slam poet, rapper and other poets all enriching my own poetic vision.

Preface

Our poetic journey begins in Tintagel, with its turquoise sea, rocky coves, rising green hills and rugged coastal cliffs. Here we gaze into this landscape oozing with Arthurian legend. Its castle ruins evoke Druid rituals and Merlin's magic. One can imagine hearing the haunting monks singing plainchant from where the old chapel used to stand.

Next, we drift into the yearly Celtic cycle to the four seasonal feasts, Samhain, or Halloween, Imbolc in February, Beltane on May Day and Lugnasadh in August. We also explore the four seasonal equinoxes; in the summer solstice we're transported into the Celtic otherworld to Stonehenge, where the rising sun brings our primitive instincts and the cosmos to life.

'Ancient River Thames' sees us make a brief visit to Roman London where Mithraism is practised in underground temples by the serpent-shaped ancient River Thames, sacred to the Celts.

Then we see how Babylon sun's symbol influenced the Celts and today's church.

Next we visit Albion and feel the presence of Gog Magog walking through the Neolithic Cornish landscape. The 'Holy Grail at Glastonbury' is the prologue to my epic poem and begins with the legend of Joseph of Arimathea, who planted his staff on Wearyall Hill. From the staff grew the Holy Thorn. A cutting of the thorn thrives and blossoms at Christmas and Easter in Glastonbury Abbey grounds. Joseph also placed the Holy Grail near a well at Chalice Hill.

The poem continues with 'The Quest of Sir Gawain', he's grieving over King Arthur's death and Merlin is trapped inside a cave. There were frequent wars between the Britons and Saxons during this period. Gawain's main concern is Morgan La Fay's powerful spell cast over Britain that touches on the eternal. Even the monks are deceived, worshipping the sun god symbol, circled round the Celtic cross on the altar. Sir Gawain's destined by knights of the round table to free the nation from this evil, and must find the Holy Grail and drink from it to receive divine power to defeat the sorceress La Fay. During his quest, he faces all kinds of trials and battles the Green Man, where he finds himself drawn into a cycle of death and rebirth. Gawain eventually ends up in the wild hunt in the Samhain with the Celtic god as the Dark Lord. He eventually finds the Holy Grail, drinks and is able to defeat the sorceress and goes on with his fellow men to defeat the invading Saxons.

Saint Etheldreda, a princess, was born in 630 in the hamlet of Exning. She inspires the next poem in this collection, Soham Monastery and Cratendune. During her youth, she used to travel in the misty and dark fens to the benighted Soham Monastery and onto a church called Cratendune, near Ely Abbey, for daily prayer. It's here that she becomes Abbess. She married Alderman Tonbert in Ely, becoming a widow soon after. Later, she remarried, to Egfrid the ruler of Northumbria, and gaining the title of Queen. After some time, Etheldreda and Egfrid agreed on a separation, as she was still a virgin and wanted to pursue the religious life.

This is followed by 'The Sacking of Soham Monastery' it was burned to the ground by the Danes in 870, in this horrific event the monks are murdered and this incident's told by Odin's two crows searching for food.

We are then taken on a raid with a Viking woman warrior, where she slaughters a holy and radiant Benedictine monk in a British monastery. She's filled with remorse and becomes a Christian. The Viking gods are furious and decide to take revenge on her. On her way home, she faces a dreadful storm and finds herself drifting into middle earth in the land of the world ash tree (Yggdrasill). She begins her perilous journey and faces the frost giants in Utgard. She escapes by sliding down the ash's root to the dark underworld in Hell. After many struggles, she reaches the Rainbow Bridge into Asgard and Valhalla. Finally, she breaks out of this demonic world of myth and soars on the astral plain into Heaven.

Now we're in New York during the thirties, where introverted Steve puts on his ritual mask, experiences his super ego and torments some gangsters as their machine gun bullets bounce off his chest. Then we move out to the prairie and join in three native American dances, the war dance capturing the rhythm of the natives' drumbeat.

We go to a nightclub bar and witness the mechanical doll's amazing dance; this is in complete contrast to the Swan Lake dance, which is graceful and dreamy. Finally, nearer to home we meet the showy rapper with his troubled soul.

In the next selection of poems, we encounter some places and events, beginning with a sea trip to Fingal's Cave and then on to a lively medieval fayre.

Next we go on a fox hunt, each stanza echoing the rhythm of the galloping horses.

The First World War frames 'The Battle of the Somme', in which the reader experiences the horrors of trench warfare. This leads onto the Second World War at Soham Station, blown to smithereens by a munitions train.

Now it's time for us to take a peep into the spiritual background of the European Union at Strasbourg, its unfinished eastern tower giving the impression that Europe's constantly evolving. The architecture depicts the foundations of ancient and modern designs in western civilisation. From Classicism to Baroque and from Galileo's to Kepler's ellipse, the transition from a static geometric mode to one showing constant motion mirrors the evolutions of institutions like the EU, which transformed from a central power to a democratic organisation, although its primary aim is to finish up as a super state and the glorification of man.

How strange this building, with all its sophistication, should end up like Bruegel's painting, 'The Tower of Babel'. Babel was an ancient city in Babylon, its people united with a single language. Nimrod the hunter decided to build a tower that would reach the heavens to worship God. However, in the end it was dedicated to the glory of man. God became concerned at the centralisation of power, so He confused the people, causing them to speak in different languages, and they were scattered to various parts of the earth. How curious the motto for the EU is: 'Many Tongues, One Voice.' In the end times, ancient Babylon's rebuilt and becomes Satan's capital city of the world.

Even more bizarre, the other half of the EU building is designed like the Roman Colosseum, known for its gruesome history, where the torturing and murdering Christians for sheer entertainment took place. Many of its emperors were under the spell of the Antichrist.

Finally, the statue of Europa riding a bull is displayed outside the EU and the Brussels parliament. The myth Greek tells that Zeus disguised himself as a dazzling white bull with horns glowing like a crescent moon and Europa rode upon his back before being plunged into the waves of the sea, where Zeus rapes her. She gave birth to a son and after her death she became the Queen of Heaven. The bull, Taurus, became a constellation in the sky.

Let us return to Babylon... Nimrod has a wife, Semiramis, who was beautiful yet corrupt, portrayed in ancient carvings and paintings with a halo of stars around her head. She became the Queen of Heaven and gave birth to a son named Tammuz, who's represented in the Roman Catholic host. Throughout the European churches, the Queen of Heaven is often depicted standing on a crescent moon and the bull is seen in other pagan religions. Emperor Charles the IV issued an edict at the Diet of Nuremburg in 1356 for the purpose of regularising the election to the throne of the empire. It was sealed with a golden bull, (Papal Bull).

Next, we confront the Four Horsemen of the Apocalypse as the harlot rides the beast during the end times. Briefly, we experience the danger of soul power and then a frightening ride through Death Valley and meet the Grim Reaper.

Then, we visit Rievaulx Abbey, where the monks engage in spiritual warfare.

Finally, we find peace in a monastery garden, where nuns singing plainchant at prime, sext, vespers and nocturns. Once again, we return to Glastonbury to the Lord's pilgrimage in England influenced by Blake's Jerusalem.

Celtic Poems

Tintagel

King Pendragon's Celtic castle,
Standing on those lofty heights,
Set in the land of Arthurian legend,
Where the turquoise sea delights;
On grey and dark green Cornish coast,
Breaking waves on rocky shore,
Haunt for many a giant and ghost,
Raging here for evermore,
Magic comes from Merlin's cave,
Travels all round in Tintagel,
Hark! The ancient voices rave,
Grip the soul like a witch's spell.

Druids in their hooded white cloaks,
Ghosting the ritual grey stone circle,
Overlooking some crooked crags,
Under the skies all red and purple.
Britons love this feast of Beltane,
Dark priests chant between the fires,
Watching faces grin in the flames,
Kindle their spirits and deep desires.

Virgin screams at that ritual knife,
And her blood drips from an altar,
Sun's appeased with innocent life,
Glows beyond the realm of nature,
In this land where gods once trod,
Power now surges from bubbling spring,

Twin-horned nature, green-leafed god,
Now appears before the Celtic King.

Epona gallops on her white horse,
Bringing out that fertile sun,
Revels in its solar force,
Now this springtime birth has come,
When a fork of lightning strikes,
Thundering dark demons wake,
Moved by these religious rites,
Ground now trembles like an earthquake.

Soaring eagle's wings outspread
Over a phantom Roman legion,
Marching feet disturb the dead,
Bring about this evil omen;
For the heavens look so bleak,
Dragon breaks free from his chains,
Down in Hell's dark dungeon deep,
Breathing out his stream of flames,
When this fiend flies high in the air,
Flapping its wings in a steady beat,
Huge eyes fixed in icy stare,
While its body glows with heat,
Nearby village mantled in mist,
Peasants huddle together indoors,
Hear this creature from the abyss,
All frozen by its deafening roars.

Monks all move in Saint Columba's
Spirit, seated together in prayer,

Chapels filled with signs and wonders,
Gold dust floating through the air,
Celtic cross's circle glows,
Piercing through the realms of time,
Holy Spirit's energy flows,
When his peace exceeds the sublime;
Candles burn on the altar so bright,
Room all scented with fragrance,
When this place bursts forth in light,
Here in the might of Christ's presence,
Holding keys of death and Hell,
Quenches, dispels the power of magic,
Makes the devils quake and quell,
From his blood and heroic spirit,
That rescues the Britons in distress,
Through his divine authority,
Overcomes the Kingdom of Darkness,
As He will for all eternity.
Monks all celebrate with songs,
Sing about his crown of thorns,
Shaking the raving devils' prongs,
That pushes back demonic storms.

Climbing sun now gleams in gold,
Along this rugged coast in Cornwall,
Glory of God enhances nature,
Blessing touches all Tintagel.

The Yearly Celtic Cycle

Village church clock begins its icy chime,
Chills the soul, now an ill wind's blowing,
Stirring up the spirits way back in time,
Come to celebrate this Feast of Samhain.
Thirteen witches astride their besom broomsticks,
At the twelfth stroke of midnight on Halloween,
Silhouetted by the moon's eclipse,
Delighted to hear some ghosts and ghouls all scream,
As they swoop down on the churchyard graves,
Laugh at skeletons shaking inside their tombs,
Where they meet a pale-faced zombie that raves,
Reveling in this place where terror looms.
Beneath the staring eyes of a screeching owl,
They turn a key to open death's dark door,
That releases some evil spirits so foul,
Finding how it makes their soul power soar,
They all engage in a dance of death,
With a demonic presence that so inspires,
They're moving around to right and to the left,
Chanting their rhymes near the blazing briars,
Watching the horned Devil in bonfire's flames,
Steps out of its centre and then bows his head,
As the moon's eclipse begins to wane,
The witches dance around with spiritual dead.

Hark the freezing winter winds do blow,
Leaving the branches with a ghostly stare,
There among the falling flakes of snow,

When Jack Frost's bite is felt in the air;
Icicles frozen on a watermill,
Under the sky's red and purple cloak,
Snow is whiter than the sheep on the hill,
Shepherd leads them down a wooded slope.
The sheep all safe in a pen, he goes to the village,
Longing for a brandy in the Queen of Hearts,
Crosses over an ancient hump-stone bridge,
Passing families in horse-drawn carts,
He sees a shadow by a village pump,
Startled when he hears an eerie voice,
A Druid's spectre near an old oak stump,
Here in the village square in this winter solstice.
Shepherd's haunted by this following dream,
Sees a silver-horned moon, lying low,
Shines on an oak's thick branches no longer green,
Although it's bearing sprigs of mistletoe,
He's sad a sickle cuts it from the bark,
With its clump of berries all sparkling white,
Moved by a ritual song playing on a harp,
Dark Moon Goddess appears in her gown of light.

Welcome to February's shining sun,
Wakes up this Celtic season of Imbolc,
Stirring infant roots in earth's wide womb,
Gives birth to scores of shivering snowdrops;
There in the winter sunshine's golden glow,
That sparks off aconites on nature's floor.
Yellow and mauve crocuses peer in the snow,
Just like a pretty maiden's pinafore;
Down by a river rushing over rocks,

Between the evergreen pines and spiky larch,
Moving through time to spring equinox,
On a sunny, breezy day in March,
Swaying a bed of dancing daffodils
And primroses and splashes of violets blue,
Lambs leap in the valleys and laughing hills,
And those budding leaves start peeping through.
Saint Brigid appears at this glorious feast,
Walking by freshwater bubbling springs,
Lovely features and a heart full of peace,
Reflecting her purity, white as an angel's wings,
And her sparkling strands of golden hair,
Her cheeks all red just like the womb of dawn,
She moves around in a light and delicate air,
Her song mingling with the birds at morn,
Arrayed there in a dazzling, long white gown,
That sudden bluish twinkle in her eyes,
Wearing a garland glowing like a crown,
She's making music with her lyre at sunrise.

Farewell to April sunshine and its showers,
Hark, the chiming church bells ringing,
The gardens smiling with their springtime flowers,
Still the cuckoo calls and songbirds singing.
Walpurgis Night brings forth its bright full moon,
Shining through the haunting atmosphere,
Witches mounted on their crooked brooms,
Sweeping over a red-faced ridge in Shropshire,
Whooshing straight down on a mountainside,
Eager to mix with demon, fiend and beast,
With ghostly hooded Druids as their guide,

There by the bonfires at this Beltane feast.
Witches summon the elves from underground
And send their magic through the air to enhance,
The energy pounding from the rocks all round,
Driving the old hags into a ritual dance,
Reaching a pitch that makes the earth vibrate.
Then they suddenly stop, all out of breath,
Find they're staring into an earthquake,
Finally meeting Satan, the master of death,
Seeing him rise up from the fires of Hell,
In lightning flashes in the bottomless pit,
Up from where his demons of darkness dwell,
Now brings life to every foul and evil spirit.

This followed by the passionate month of May,
With red and white may blossom in its prime,
Rippling streams go merrily on their way,
Through flowery meadows, looking divine,
Where happy couples walk together and laugh,
Arm in arm as youthful lovers should,
Over the stiles along a winding path,
That ends up by a maze in a bluebell wood.

A gathering crowd soon find their spirits soar,
Seeing sunlit streets all spring alive,
With hawthorn sprigs hanging on each door
And the antlered Morris dancers arrive;
With bells all jingling round their stamping feet,
Welcome a galloping clumsy hobby horse,
Violinist hyping up the rhythmic beat,
That touches on the power in nature's force.

May Queen leads the pied piper's procession,
All in step and dragging hawthorn boughs,
Along a dusty road, singing a folk song,
Finding their feelings even more aroused
At the maypole dancers on high field green,
Later they drive a wicker man, Green George,
And symbolically drown him in a stream,
That is running behind a blacksmith's forge.
They all cheer at the death of the May King,
Surprised how those flowery meadows shine,
The way its spirit touches everything,
It pierces the realms of nature and through time.

Midsummer solstice on Salisbury Plain,
Ringed green mounds straight from the Iron Age,
Where primitive rhythms hammer through the brain,
When the rising sun's so red with rage,
While the body absorbs its solar power,
Shudders at blood dripping from altar stone,
Feeling a sweeping force that seems to devour,
Make the darkest depths of the psyche groan;
Seeing spiral circles spinning with a flare,
Entering into the realm of nature's dark door,
Meeting with those princes and powers of the air,
That fills the atmosphere around with awe.
Now the haunted heavens rumble and roll,
Thunder crashes, echoes and it booms,
Lightning flashes, raising the height of the soul,
Ancestral spirits spring from their tombs.
Terrifying sound from their dreaded feet,
Conjuring up those screaming souls in Hell,

All under control from a demonic beat,
That grips the whole of Stonehenge in its spell.
Between upright and overhanging stones,
Rising sun now shines in a circle of gold,
Sending forth its wavering cosmic rays,
Revealing all the magic and mysteries of old,
Going round and round in the mind like a maze.
Ancient priests embark on astral flight,
Soaring round their circle in eternity,
Meet with Satan as the Angel of Light.

The reapers rising with the reddening dawn,
These country folk from around the shire,
Watching solar spirit swaying the corn
And the sun's rim red as a forge fire,
They welcome this hot season of Lughnasadh,
As they sharpen their scythes on a whetted stone,
Fear the omen where scores of ravens' nag.
There under the sun in its brilliant blue dome,
Their flashing scythes sweeping through a golden field,
Bodies tanned in the shimmering heat haze,
How they sweat and toil for their yearly yield,
All bent on this back-breaking work for days.

Deep in the wood under a harvest moon,
Horned dancers go round and round in a ring,
Overcome with a haunting sense of doom,
There before a gnarled old oak hit by lightning.
They meet with the antlered god, Hunter Hearne,
Then dance around the old oak anti-clockwise,
Stirring up their pagan passions that burn,

Seeing how the fire lights up in their eyes,
Moving around so wild like fiends possessed,
Startled when the oak tree bursts into flames,
Surprised by their gods that manifest,
The nature Celtic god Cernunnos who reigns,
They watch him glow green in this fire festival,
And go on dancing until the morning light,
There before the bearded sun god Lugh,
That soon heightens this religious rite.

The workers gather in harvest with strength of an ox,
Have furrowed the fields with horses and plough,
Here in time with autumn equinox,
When the leaves start turning on the bough.
Fruitfulness will soon flood the market places
And stalls decorated with all its trimmings,
With sparkling fruits among the smiling faces,
End this season with orange prize pumpkins.

White bearded man kicking up autumn leaves,
Lay there like a quilted eiderdown,
Beneath the golden branches of the trees,
Among a feast of red and copper brown,
The man puffing from his pipe and, out of breath,
Coughing and spluttering from his tobacco smoke,
Saddened by the summer's long lingering death,
That the last few fluttering leaves evoke.

Ancient River Thames

Sun sets on the River Thames,
Fiery bright red serpent raves,
Wakes the spirits way back in time,
Rising from their ancient graves,
River keeps on rolling along,
Mystery thrives and mist comes down
And this slithering river flows,
Here through dear old London Town.

Its water's weave by Parliament,
At the twelfth stroke of Big Ben,
Fading chime that chills the soul,
Coincide with Celtic Samhain.
Tidal wave and waters heave,
Livens spirits' deadly dance,
Moonlight spreads its silver beams,
These macabre moods enhance.

Celtic past alive and well,
Underground laid those ritual bones,
Ghostly hooded Druids chanting,
Echo through the catacombs.
A voice cries from Hallows Hill,
Buried skull of Bran's white head,
Glowing on those foggy waters,
Stir deep beneath that river bed.

Boadicea, a British Queen,
Rides her chariot through the air,
Fights against the might of Rome,
Victory through her sacred hare;
Gog Magog with burning torches,
Tread the street with ancient feet,
Leads procession back in time,
There in tune with river's heartbeat.

Morning sun on the River Thames,
Fiery bright red serpent raves,
Wakes the spirits from years ago,
Now return to their ancient graves,
River keeps on rolling along,
Mystery thrives and mist comes down,
Ghostly ferryman sings his song,
Here in dear old London Town.

Roman London

Years ago, on this island of Great Britain,
Roman legions marched down the street,
Through the Romano-Celtic Londinium,

The echo from Gog Magog's ancient feet,
Struck at the Druidic magic London stone,
Its secrets speak through London's heartbeat.

Beneath the soaring eagle's symbol of Rome,
Its Mithraicism practiced half-underground,
In a temple its ghosts heighten the tone,

Once worshipped that golden sun so round,
Sparkled on the Celtic River Thames,
Slithered like a serpent through London Town;

That bore a hallmark in time that never ends.

Babylon in Celtic and Catholic Culture

Ritual rising in red and golden dawn,
Open eyelids of the waking morn,
Celtic tribesmen in a trance and stare,
Fear the tension in the trembling air.
In the heart of a grove among some oaks,
Druids gather in drooping hooded cloaks,
Calling up spirits from a raging river,
There beneath moon just like a slither.
Maidens' fingers plucking strings on their lyres,
Worship before those blazing Beltane fires.
Giants and dwarfs come up from underground,
When newborn sun appears all red and round,
Shining out its golden spokes like a wheel,
Celts all dance round in a circle with zeal,
Finding themselves in tune with earth's heartbeat,
Feeling the fertility with their frenzied feet
And become one with their gods in soul power,
Forces beyond nature that seek to devour.
Heightened by a human sacrifice,
Virgin screaming at the top of her voice,
Touches Taranis, who fills the sky with thunder,
Flashes over a blood-stained stone altar,
Makes the priests' and people's passions burn,
Masked and wear the antlers of hunter Hearn;
Bow before the sun, their source of life,
Babylonian religion here is rife;
How it preys around just like a vulture,
Swoops through centuries from culture to culture,

Seeking out death and continues its search,
Settles its claws in cathedral and church,
Proud, his false prophet sits on his throne,
There inside the Vatican City of Rome.
Sun shines through its window in the east,
And its shadow falls on a Jesuit priest,
Holding up a sun god in the host,
Tammuz a counterfeit and demonic ghost,
His mother standing on a crescent moon,
There beneath her feet her worshippers swoon,
Look to the Queen of Heaven, wearing a crown,
Spreads out her hands, adorned in bright blue gown,
Believers gripped by the Babylonian past,
That is hidden by a Christian mask.

Albion

Our pirate ship drops anchor on the shores of Cornwall,
We're stunned by its breathtaking, rugged coast,
And feel dark Merlin's presence, weaving his spell,
Then find that ancient Albion is our host.
We watch those waters hissing through the caves,
Where the ancient voices sound so eerie,
Their faces flashing on crest of rolling waves,
How they break upon that shore in fury.

Now we walk in the footsteps of Gog Magog,
In this land we feel Albion's heartbeat,
Underneath a blanket of swirling fog,
That haunting sound of ancestral dancing feet,
With its rhythms and primeval force,
We're stirred and it echoes through the age-old hills,
Then hear the hoof beats from Epona's white horse,
We're thrust in a Neolithic mood that chills,
Seeing nature gods wake from the other side
And that spirit of Albion brings us alive.

The Holy Grail at Glastonbury

Prologue

The Jewish nation was held captive in Babylon
And influenced the Catholic and Celtic culture,
Eventually reaching the churches in Great Britain,

How it preyed around like a starving vulture,
Soared and sought to quench eternal flame,
Through the ages and never failed to allure.

Some gathering Druids held a feast at Beltane,
And watched, close by a saint, there on a ferry,
He carried Christ's chalice of suffering and pain.

Arrived at edge of a lake near Glastonbury,
This holy man was Joseph of Arimathea,
Here on a mission to set this country free.

The man possessed the vision of a seer,
And planted his pilgrim's staff on Wearyall Hill,
That blossoms at Easter and Christmas every year.

This miraculous sign would prove to be God's will,
When Joseph put the Grail in a bubbling spring,
Whoever drunk from it would conquer all ill.

Its finder would present the perfect offering,
And know the prophet's purpose would prevail,
When he heard those holy angels sing;

And Britain will receive a future blessing from Israel.

The Quest of Sir Gawain

Sir Gawain was a noble and a valiant knight,
Grieved how the other knights ranted and raved,
How Arthur's death had put him in this plight,

When darkness fell on Britain, it looked so grave,
And on the benighted castle here at Camelot,
Lamented that Merlin's body was found in a cave,

Excalibur drawn out from a magic rock,
Was grasped by a hand from Lady of the Lake,
That left all Arthur's knights in a state of shock.

They realized the time had come to make or break,
And face the evil sorceress Morgan La Fay,
With her warlike soul that's full of hate.

Although he'd challenge her every step of the way,
He found her hard heart black as a raven forsook,
That made him restless, throughout night and day,

Then he saw her dancing the Druid's Foot,
High up on the Tor from the middle of a maze,
He embraced terror when the aged earth shook,

Under the moon, his hopes were almost erased,
At her powerful spell, he saw the way she gnashed
Her teeth at the Beltane Feast with bonfires ablaze,

And a firebird rose up from the ashes,
He knew her magic raised the mythical phoenix,
Saw rivers and streams give off lightning flashes,

Aware it the moved the dark beast chained in abyss,
He looked to the future when it would reign in Babylon,
With the false prophet during apocalypse,

There in darkness he yearned for the rising sun,
Realized she summoned the underworld god, Arawn,
And he brought death from the satanic kingdom.

Some figures approached him in the dark red dawn,
Heard Druids droning inside oak tree grove,
Surprised by walking dead that chilled the morn.

Then he watched the Master of Death behove,
The sorceress to attack mankind's spirit,
There beneath those skies of yellow and mauve,

He thought about the six hundred and sixty-six,
How her sorcery touched the end of time,
And wondered how on earth he's going to stop it.

Later he joined the monks all gathered at prime,
Before sun symbol round their Celtic cross,
Appalled how they worshipped it in riddles and rhyme.

He's saddened how their spiritual path was lost,
Their cowls cast shadows in their candlelit monastery,
Knew the Devil dragged up all this dross.

He realized how it clouded their chivalry,
The round table glowed with signs from zodiac,
The stars influenced by Babylon's astrology.

The knights now faced an all-out Saxon attack,
The sorceress also dimmed their eternal flame,
It seemed there wouldn't be any way back.

All the fingers pointed to Sir Gawain,
To search and drink from Saviour's Holy Grail,
For he's the only one who's born again.

This knight sent on a quest that mustn't fail,
A golden lion blazon on his green shield,
He rode his stallion through a shadowy vale.

The soft sun smiled, he came to a flowery field,
And heard some trumpets blow at a summer tourney,
As for jousting he'd never been forced to yield.

This steadfast, lively Irishman, often merry,
He loved music and sung along with his harp,
Sometimes he'd fall into a state of reverie.

A noble character, always played his part,
Courteous to the ladies, yet prone to lust,
And sometimes rage would cloud his loving heart.

He continued on his journey until dusk,
And saw some blazing torches in a forest,
Then faced the antlered nature god Cernunnos,

And he felt fear well up inside his breast,
This god all clad in leaves from head to toe,
And he found this meeting hard to digest.

After a while he decided to go with the flow,
And from that moment he seemed to lose his reason,
Now linked to Celtic cycle, it filled him with woe,

That took him on a journey through each season,
Then caught a glimpse of the Celtic god's young bride,
A raven-haired moon goddess with rounded bosom,

And he foolishly looked to them as his guide,
Surprised when the god turned into a stag,
It's powerful magic that took him for a ride.

He saw her change to a crow and heard it nag,
There among the silver birches and ferns,
And he found that time just seemed to drag.

Deep inside he felt his passions burn,
Now he'd been influenced by their power,
Dark elves haunted him at every turn.

Here in this place that threatened to devour,
Above he saw a silver spinning wheel,
Among the starry sky at this midnight hour,

A naked goddess appeared and made him reel,
How her dark brown eyes touched on his desire,
And his quest now seemed to lose its appeal.

He was delighted, his senses blazed like fire,
Realized there'd be a heavy price to pay,
That his total submission would prove to be dire.

Somehow, he mounted his horse and went on his way,
Then he saw her change to a giant spider,
He whipped his horse to a gallop, began to pray.

It seemed impossible to avoid her,
Felled from his steed and covered in silver thread,
Repulsed by her body, bristling in black fur,

Now he's caught up in her silken web,
All numbed and unable to move any limb,
He felt her vicious bite and found he bled.

He cried for help for falling into sin,
Sensed she'd lunge in swiftly for the kill,
And he felt his strength return within.

Now freed, he thrust his flashing sword with skill,
That pierced her flesh until it oozed with gore,
That robbed her of her meal and wicked will,

Then he saw her disappear with a roar,
Carried on his journey to a moonlit lake,
It looked so peaceful and calm, but he felt unsure.

When a ferryman appeared so full of heartache,
And he noticed his furtive look as he moored,
Alarmed his horse that started to neigh and shake.

Somehow, he managed it to step on board
The ferry and he travelled on Lake Avalon,
Moments on the waters, the thunder roared.

Soon the lake became like a bubbling cauldron,
The faces of the furies lit up in the clouds,
And he heard the beating wings of a dragon.

It seemed that heaven was covered with a shroud,
His ferry forced towards dark Witch's Isle,
He perished the thought of meeting this evil crowd.

Now washed ashore, having survived this trial,
He faced a dark-haired woman with lunar lips,
Stunned by her beauty and bewitching smile,

With her firm white breast and slimline hips,
But he sensed such evil from that twitch
In her eyes and the power at her fingertips,

He plucked up courage to shun this wicked witch,
But not before she's sent him fast asleep,
Although he'd almost escaped without a glitch,

But he'd slept through time without a peep,
Awoke and never saw the summer so green,
Not-so if his horse hadn't licked his cheek.

The hedges, trees and meadows glowed like a dream,
The silver stream weaving along in zest,
He thought the energy came from the Summer Queen,

Appeared all garlanded with flowers, in her emerald dress,
With glittering falling tresses of golden hair,
He was stunned by her figure and rounded breast.

He watched her slay the Green Man without a care,
Realized this was the season she must reign,
All around he saw her sparkle and flare.

Although her charms played havoc with his brain,
He must pull himself together and move on,
How her influence filled his heart with shame.

Then he felt a prod from the Devil's prong,
And faced a dragon, crouched down by the shore,
Could this be the challenge to right his wrong?

The way to open yet another door,
Soon he found himself fighting against its fire,
Protected by his shield, he came back for more.

After a while, his chances proved to be dire,
And he began to think his quest would fail,
When all his best efforts seemed to tire,

Until he swung his sword and cut off its tail,
And the creature let out a bitter cry,
As its body went from red to pale

And flapped its wings, rising up high in the sky,
This victory filled his heart with belief and hope,
Delighted the Devil's plans had gone awry.

It seemed he no longer bore a heavy yoke,
Once again, he jumped onto the ferry,
And the ferryman soon cast off his rope.

At last he arrived at a quay near Glastonbury,
Startled by the withered hand on his shoulder,
Those evil voices that came from the monastery,

The hermit's grim words made his anger smoulder,
And Morgan La Fay's influence on people and priest,
And the atmosphere seemed that much colder.

All the shouting that came from a pagan feast,
Down in the village that spread like a plague,
Some died from Balor's deadly eye in the east.

The way ahead looked so bleak and vague,
He and the hermit decided to wrestle in prayer,
For a while inside his firelit cave.

At evening, he saw a passing medieval fair,
The harvest fertility rites at Lughnasadh,
Later, he felt that bite from the autumn air.

He saw the Summer Queen's sparkle retard,
Her glittering hair now hung there all lank,
How tyrant time exposed her pagan facade.

He no longer saw flowers all lacing the bank,
Only those bodies slain from Balor's glance,
Some lay in the ditches and dykes all dank.

Now he'd seize this moment in time to advance,
When the people's spirit reached low ebb,
Realized after a while he'd taken a chance.

Saw that Cernunnos had come back from the dead,
Rose as Dark Lord leading the Samhain Hunt,
Chased a bristling wild boar running ahead,

Somehow, he found himself riding out in front,
And he's under a nature god's dark spells,
With demons mounted on goats, all gave a grunt.

He's terrified on hearing Hell's rumbling bowels,
And rode his skeleton horse on its fiery plains,
And choked violently on its brimstone smells,

He's scorched by its unquenchable flames,
Tormented from the tortured suffering souls,
That screamed in terror, rattling their rusty chains.

Almost deafened from the thunder that rolls,
He realized the cloven hoofs had quickened in pace,
And passed faces grinning from totem poles,

Shocked by Satan stoking his fiery furnace,
Saw his horns light up in a lightning strike,
Now his eyes are opened on this chase

Of death and finds himself on a moonlit night,
And noticed some Druids in a wooded gill,
Danced with spirits in this pagan rite,

When he rode swiftly down Wearyall Hill,
He caught sight of Joseph's glowing footprints,
And he followed them to a rushing rill.

He left his panting horse and stood convinced,
When golden light blazed from the Holy Grail,
Although its powerful presence made him flinch.

When he drank he knew he would prevail,
And grasped his sword that gleamed in eternal power,
Found it even brightened up his chainmail.

How long he'd waited for this crucial hour,
Surprised he's travelling on the astral plain,
And heard the sorceress scream from a castle tower,

Then they clashed and she fought like a woman insane,
Attempted to slice through his silver chord,
He proved too strong and her power began to wane.

All the people were freed, he praised the Lord,
Then found himself on a raging battlefield,
There at the ready with his drawn, glowing sword.

He faced the Saxons locked from shield to shield,
Watched wheels of fire all hurtling down a slope,
And certain this would make the enemy yield.

Now he's pleased the Britons are full of hope,
When all the Saxon ranks were split asunder,
And knew deep down their spirits were broke

When the Celtic chariots sounded like thunder,
Their flashing spears and swords wreaked havoc,
Soon the Saxons were buried six foot under.

The Celtic gods no longer divided the kingdom,
Sir Gawain's prayers all ended with an amen.

Anglo Saxon and
Viking Poems

Soham Monastery and Cratendune

Etheldreda so elated in her Exning village,
In her free flowing, ruby red mantle,
Its border embroidered in burning gold,
With her pale blue, three-quarter length gown,
The purity of her presence in a princess's crown,
With her fine features and flowing flaxen hair,
Sparkling so softly in the summer air,
She breathes in by some bubbling springs,
As she goes through the glorious green meadows,
Singing sacred songs and strumming her lyre,
Lying there with lambs, she looks so sweet,
Slips into slumber and starts to dream.
One winter's night she wends her way to Soham
Monastery, mumbling on this moonlit night,
Enhanced by hoar frost on the hawthorn briars,
She paces along a pagan path of gems,
Sparkling like scattered speckles of gold,
Beneath those shining stars sprinkling above.
She moves by the Mere's mystical sea,
Circles round this Celtic cauldron of plenty,
Bubbling and boiling and bursting with energy,
She sees how it steams and soars in soul power,
Evoking enchanting elves in the fire,
Mingling in the magic on these misty waters,
Drawn by a demonic droning 'Druid's choir,'
Surprised by spirits springing out a spiral portal,
She's reviled at this ritual of the rising dead,
Dancing the dance of death on the dark waters,

Flickering in fury in flashes of light,
Weaving and whining with will of the wisps,
Cohort and celebrate on this Celtic Samhain.

She wanders wearily to a walled moat,
Crossing over a wide wooden bridge,
Moving among those grey monastic buildings,
Then roams around a Roman tower,
Marvels at this medieval monastery so dark,
Enthralled as she enters its English oak door,
Stepping so silently on a grey stone floor,
Lucid candlelight looming on long north transept,
She meets with the monks at midnight mass,
Bowing with Benedictines before a Celtic cross,
Eating emblems and exalting the Lord,
Sipping from that suffering cup of wine,
That becomes the broken body and blood of Christ.

Uplifted she leaves and loses her way,
Frightened and further on finds a ferryman,
Hiding himself in his hideous hooded cloak,
She steps onto the raft and stands at the back,
Watching him plunge his punting pole in the water,
Shaking the sedge and swamps at the edge,
Bogeymen bouncing on those bubbling bogs and
Ghosts and ghouls glimmering from the reeds,
Thunder from Thor as he throws his hammer,
That drives her through a darkening door in the past.
She winces at Woden's wild wicked hound,
Leering there and lights up in the lightning flashes,
She's so daunted by this black dog of death with saucer

Eyes, glaring, glowing and gloating in evil,
Breathing brimstone from his blazing nostrils,
That's fueled from that fiery furnace in Hell.
She sees some saliva slopping from its jaws,
Terrified its teeth will tear her to pieces
From limb to limb and leave her for dead,
She clutches at her cross and calls on Christ's name,
And that crying hound collapses and crumbles to dust,
Blown on breath of a breeze, bellowing in the night,
Woeful Woden wanders on his way with a groan.

She's ferried by the ferryman further on,
Drifting deep into a dark dripping cave,
Slithering on the serpentine River Styx,
She's frightened by flashing faces on the wall,
So grim with their glimmering green eyes,
As she meanders through a monster's open mouth,
Journeying and jolting into the jaws of Hell.
She's rattled by the ravenous river running faster,
Gorging and hears gurgling in its gigantic belly,
Beneath a bulging black beating heart,
Shocked by scores of souls all screaming in agony,
Railing at the reverberating rumbles of thunder
And lightning flashing on that luminous lake of fire,
She's whipped round in a whirring whirlpool,
Spinning and spewing her safely up above.
She's so relieved the raft reaches the bank,
Steps off and scampers up Stuntney Hill,
Onwards and over to the other side,
Where she boards a barge below,
And being rowed on the rippling River Ouse,

Mirrored by moonlight for miles on end,
She's roused by the raven-haired river goddess,
With her beautiful body and shapely bosom,
Welling up from this watery womb with a twist,
Watches her whisked away and whining in the fog,
Chanting for Cernunnos the chief Celtic god,
She stares at an antlered stag standing on the bank,
Beneath the black and bare branches of the oaks,
She's amazed at moonlight on the mistletoe,
Bearing its beaming berries so white,
The raucous ravens raising the pitch,
White bull's blood brimming from an altar,
Druids doing their dance of death
And waking the weird and wonderful white goddess,
Standing so serenely on sacred ground,
Among the flames of fire flaring up in fury,
Where soaring spirits are spooking the air,
When she kneels in the keel to pray,
All the foul fiendish faces fade away.

At last, she lands on the little isle,
Finds herself in a flourishing fishery at Braham,
Saunters by several Saxon buildings,
Topped with triangular thatched roofs,
She's troubled by a troll as she trudges up hill,
Reaching a Roman road so alone,
Sensing sneering spectres in the dark,
Bustling in the bushes and brambles that shake,
She's alerted by a legion of Roman soldiers,
Moving through the moonlight with marching feet,
And daunted by their deadly demonic beat;

She sees some sinister shadowy wings
Of an eagle, evoking the evil empire spirit,
That sends shudders straight down her spine.
She comes to her Christian church at Cratendune,
Bows before the burning candles and cross,
And her face reflects in its flickering light,
This lively lady so loyal and loving in virtue,
Her spirit and soul soaring in the sanctuary,
In holiness with a halo above her head,
Burning so brightly in brilliant gold,
She's devoted to a divine dove hovering,
Feeling its fiery falling tongues,
There in the presence of this Prince of Peace.
She wanders to the window and witnesses this vision,
Fenland mist is moving like a mighty sea,
Abbey's anchored like an ark on a hill,
With shafts of light streaming from its Saxon arches,
Its radiance rises and reaches to the heavens,
Absorbed by anthems from an angelic host,
Cherubims charging in their chariots of fire,
Soaring seraphims simmering in light,
Elated by an enormous circle of emerald green,
She's overcome by this offering from an open heaven;
Looks at a ladder leading up to its heights,
Glimpses the glory of God on His throne,
His presence pouring out prophetic fire,
Assures she'll be Abbess in the abbey at Ely.
She's comforted by the craftsman's creative skill,
From the perfect picturesque pastures in Heaven,
There in this lofty light from the New Jerusalem.

The Sacking of Soham Monastery

Odin's two crows fly over a meadow,
And one pipes up and says to the other,
'Where shall we find food for tomorrow?'
'A feast on dead man's flesh, my brother,'
But first, we'll roost before it's dark,
Then rise up with the screeching owl,
That time will come to make our mark,
The sign will be Old Shuck's howl.

We feel the fury in angry clouds,
Its awesome power is sheer delight,
And see those Norse gods arouse
Stark terror on this winter's night;
We'll see how Odin's black horse moves,
Across a threatening stormy sky,
The beating from its striding hooves,
That bright red glint in our master's eye,
Wearing a grin upon his face,
We'll hear him blow his battle horn,
And his hounds' unholy sounds
Will pierce and herald the rising dawn.

We both see Thor release his hammer,
Feel the heavens shiver and shake,
From peals of thunder and streaks of lightning,
That makes the earth bright as daybreak.
We'll see the Valkyries with their spears,
Show up our plumage in their fire,

And hear their cries ring in our ears,
Echo across this Saxon shire.

Then we'll watch their dragon ships,
Their men all heaving on their oars,
We'll follow their creaking vessel's wide wake,
Hear water lap the Fenland shore.
We'll swoop straight down on lonely Soham
Monastery, overlooking the Mere,
We'll caw outside its frosted window,
And know those monks will quake in fear.
We'll hear them chant in the sanctuary,
There in the presence of the Lord,
We'll see those Danes burst in through the door
And cut them all down with the sword.

Now the grey stone floor runs with blood,
We hear the restless heavens roll,
And see them praise their pagan gods,
And bow before a bearded troll.
We'll wait until those flames die down,
When it's morning we'll find our food,
We'll spread our wings and glide around,
Then feed on flesh beneath the rood.

The Haunted Viking Longship

Sailing on board my new boat in the Hebrides,
Passing the isles of those surging seas,
Find I'm travelling way back in the past,
Facing a Viking longship's red-striped mast,
Hear its drumbeats and its rhythmic oars,
Shake at the dragon's demonic roars,
Breathing out treacherous streams of fire,
I'm caught up in this dark vision, so dire,
Driven along in this howling tempest,
Reeling around on those waves of unrest,
Then I look up in a rolling black sky,
Lit by Odin's huge red glowing eye,
I'm in a sweat and it heightens my fears,
Seeing the Valkyries' flaming giant spears,
Lashing straight out with their lightning whips,
Shows up the shields on the sides of the ship,
Catching a glimpse of its ghostly crew,
And I'm all worked up in a hell of a stew,
Cursing the pair of the Norse god's crows,
Now I seem to be gripped in death's throes.
Then so relieved at a lull in the storm,
How it all fades in the light of the dawn.

A Viking Woman Warrior

Solvig, a Viking woman warrior,
Sat by a crackling fire,
Among the feasting, drunken crowd,
Sung and strummed her lyre.
Such lovely sounds came from her voice,
Went soaring through the air,
Her coppery hair glittered so bright,
Fell on her bosom fair.

Next morning, she boarded her ship,
Soon left her rugged coast,
Ventured on a calm blue sea,
With light as pale as a ghost.
She loved the way the fleet of ships,
Cut through that rough North Sea,
Weighed anchor in an English cove,
That led to a Saxon Abbey.

Now fully-armed with sword and shield,
She stepped on to the shore,
Roused by the sound of a battle horn,
Burst in through an abbey door.
Once inside, she ran amok,
Like fury with her flashing sword,
In a dying monk's eyes, she saw
The glory of the Lord.

Somehow this vision pierced her soul,
And filled her heart with wonder,
Worth more than gold and silver chalices,
She disregarded the plunder.
There among the roaring flames,
She wept a bowlful of tears,
In the presence of the Lord,
Love swept away her fears.

After she received His guidance,
Provoked a Viking curse,
She hurried back to her fleet of ships,
All prepared for the worst.
The howling heavens turned pitch black,
Angel of Death swung his scythe,
She saw her warriors struck down dead,
And she stood there petrified.

The flashing heavens as bright as day,
She forged her way through this storm,
Heard Thor's rattling chariot wheels,
And Odin blowing his horn,
Followed by his howling hounds,
She wrestled with the billows,
Rose to heights and down to the depths,
Here on the verge of death throes.

She saw the Valkyries in their helmets,
Wielding their fiery spears,
Mounted on their skeleton steeds,
That enhanced her fears.

She saw the leafy boughs fill the skies,
Sprout from the wide world ash,
And Thor's hammer whizzed through the air,
Fast as a lightning flash.

Way yonder loomed a strange island,
She stared at its ancient shores,
Found her ship drawn to it,
A force seemed to pull on her oars.
Once on land she followed a path,
Almost devoid of hope,
Through a valley on middle earth,
What dark terrors it evoked.

As she trudged beneath a bridge,
Met some peeping witch trolls,
And crossed a dried-up riverbed,
All full of travellers' skulls.
Then she heard their thunderous feet,
When those fiends gave chase,
She found the ground began to shake,
And she quickened her pace.

She bolted over a stone-clad wall,
Fell in some drifting snow,
She stood there shivering with cold,
Wondering which way to go.
She wandered in a white wonderland,
Here in this region of Utgard,
She heard a group of grumbling giants,
Near lakes that had frozen hard.

At last she came to a sunless sea,
Where she jumped in a boat,
Thrown around on restless waters,
She barely kept afloat.
Then she faced the serpent Midgard,
That rose from the depths of the sea,
And she found it swallowed her whole,
That pleased the god Loki.

She wriggled around in the monster's throat,
Struck it with sword in hand,
Until she made the creature choke,
It spewed her out on land.
Once more she faced the winter weather,
Ran through an ancient forest,
Haunted by Fenrir, that wolf so foul,
That roamed from east to west.

She jumped into a bubbling well,
Slid down an ash's root,
Mocked by Mimir, a bearded giant,
When she passed that brute,
With her heart thumping in fear,
So scared by its evil laugh,
She plunged further into the darkness,
There on a perilous path.

Here she came to a fiery cave,
So deep there underground,
And faced the fearsome guard dog Garm,
The large and hunched-up hound.

Everywhere she heard it howling,
And cursed that dreadful dog,
Heard gnawing at the ash's roots
She faced a demon Nidhogg.

She came to a place of many rivers,
Bubbling there like cauldrons,
Emitting scores of fiery serpents,
Their eyes glowed just like demons.
Then she hopped on to a boat,
There on the water that delves
Down to a land that's full of terror,
Here she met the dark elves.

Then she fell into another river,
Carried way back in time,
To a place with primordial feel,
All covered in layers of rime.
In the south were flying embers,
Where she saw the black one,
Among the fire with his flaming sword,
That shone bright as the sun.

Under her feet the earth gave way,
She came to the gates of Hell,
Creaking sound from its rusty hinges,
Met by a woman so foul,
She followed her over a hump-stone bridge,
Into the land of the dead,
It almost drained her will to live,
But she saw her chance ahead.

When she made footholds with an axe,
Climbed up the ash's trunk,
To middle earth's underground
Caves and off she jumped.
There she heard a hammer's rhythm,
That made the anvil ring,
She watched the dwarfs temper a spear,
Then cool it in a spring.

When she saw some snarling dwarfs,
Took to her heels in flight,
Through a labyrinth of caves,
She ran towards the light.
At last she arrived on middle earth,
And received a shock,
Saw the thatched-roof buildings flattened,
All smote with Ragnarok.

Smack in the centre of a meadow,
She climbed a rainbow bridge,
Ascended to the heights of Asgard,
With Valhalla on the ridge,
A forest floor in red and gold,
She loved its leaves so green,
Underneath a brilliant blue sky,
That further fired her dreams.

The grandeur of five hundred doors,
She entered the wide great hall,
Gleaming shields lit its roof,
Swords all shone on each wall.

She stormed up spiral grey stone steps,
That led to a great high tower,
Where she saw Odin's huntsmen,
There in a mood to devour.

She saw the sun blaze in a chariot,
Being chased by wolves,
All around the heavens thundered,
At the sound of horses' hoofs,
Then she jumped in the moon's chariot,
Its fate was just the same,
When it smashed through Ymir's skull,
It rode on the astral plain.

In this place in the universe,
Where angels and demons warred,
When she rose in Heaven's tunnel,
She found her spirit soared.
Birds sang sweeter than in spring,
She felt an angel's presence,
Meadows humming in harmony,
Their fragrance rose like incense.

She's so moved by celestial choirs,
The holy city enthrals,
Diamonds that sparkled in a stream,
That power from waterfalls.
She saw swords flash like lightning,
Cherubims' chariots of fire,
Thundering round a sapphire sea,
Here she met the Messiah.

There she heard monks in a monastery,
Singing alleluia,
Everywhere the theme resounds,
All voices near and far.
There among the shining faces,
She met that murdered monk,
Now glorified in the heights of Heaven,
She hit the earth with a bump.

She landed back on her Viking ship,
Faced Thor's bolt of lightning,
With Viking ghosts all around her,
And found it all so frightening.
She jumped into the raging sea,
When her ship caught fire,
Soon engulfed in sheets of flame,
Burned like a funeral pyre.

Finally, she washed up on the shore,
After all her toil,
And so glad the soles of her feet,
Now trod on English soil,
She prayed and God gave her
An English-speaking tongue,
And He guided her to a monastery,
Here her new life had begun.

Viking Fire Festival

After nightfall, a rocket whizzes in the sky,
Booms and sprinkles stars and forms a fountain on high,
Folk with burning torches, marching down the street,
All in step with pipers and a drummer's beat.
Enter that time when Vikings ruled on Shetland Isle,
Snaking half a mile behind the Guizer Jarl,
And he stands inside his Viking longship with pride,
Uses memories from the past as his visual guide,
Wears his steel-winged helmet and in battle dress,
With his sword and shield, a hero bent on conquest.
Floki sails through uncharted seas in vast wild ocean,
Finding new lands that fill his heart with emotion,
How he rejoices and then revels in yesterday's yore,
When his ship returns home with a rapturous roar,
Hears the blacksmith's hammer, going about his craft,
Watches maidens dyeing their gowns and having a laugh,
By the long-thatched dwellings, nestled in the toft,
Underneath the mountains green and grey aloft,
Welcomes rising red sun from its bed at daybreak,
That casts Odin's dark red spear across the lake.

Jarl Squad all bent on dragging the ship along,
Striking up and singing the 'Up Helly Aa' song,
How this festival of fire ignites their spirit and soul,
Sail their ship in the past, right where those billows roll,
Facing up to a chilling north-easterly breeze,
Ride over the breakers of the seething seas,
Wonder if their creaking ship can take the strain,

There in driving, freezing, stinging drops of rain,
Asking themselves if they will survive this stormy blast,
There beneath the red-and-white striped reeling mast,
With sheer willpower, curse the wind and heaving waves;
Stern sinks lower with prow of the dragon's head raised,
Lightning flashes on the row of warriors' shields,
Now they're shaking from the clapping thunder peals.
They hear Valkyries' horses in the heavens above,
And Thor hurls his hammer with a mighty thud,
Lights up like day, echoes like a thunderbolt,
They wake from this nightmare and come to a halt.

Gathering crowds and all the torchbearers rally,
Circle and singing 'Up Helly Aa' around the galley,
Once again, a rocket whooshes into the air,
Bangs and it flashes in a violent light blue flare,
Guizer Jarl leaves his ship, as a solo bugle sounds,
Summons the heathen spirit that seems to know no bounds.
Guizers throw their torches and set the ship on fire,
Bursting into flames just like a funeral pyre,
Burns and crackles in fury, consumes the dragon's head,
People sing a solemn requiem for the dead,
Know this ship will turn into a pile of ashes.
They see the Valkyries swoop as the thunder crashes,
Come for long-dead heroes from old battlefields,
Into Valhalla under a roof of gleaming shields,
Walls of swords and spears – what a sight to behold!
Gazing at a forest garden in red and gold,
They're amazed at this grandeur, captured in the skies,
And the Viking ships, seen in morning sunrise.

Music and Dance

The Mask

Steve finds a green ritual mask in a river,
See his bones, how they shake and they shiver,
There in his apartment in the room at the top,
Puts on his mask and receives a great shock.
Stares in his mirror that hangs on the wall,
Reflecting an ego that conquers all,
Thinks he's so smart and he's kind of cute,
Here in black shoes and an emerald-green suit.
Venturing out on a New York street,
Knowing deep down he's in for a treat,
Walking along in his trilby grey hat,
Eyes all ablaze like a smart black cat,
Popping right out at this glorious brunette,
Making his hairs stand on the back of his neck.
Captures a glimpse of her beautiful breast,
Thumping red heart jumps right out of his chest,
Follows her into a rowdy night club bar,
Where he'd become a young superstar.
Clippety-clop with hypnotic swift steps,
Ritual dance that soon reaches the depths,
Flashes around with his frenzied feet,
Smack in the rhythm with the jazz band's beat.
Having his dance with a gangster's young babe,
Faces his henchman six-foot tough wild Abe.
Sees the bullets from Machine Gun Kelly,
How they bounce straight back off his belly,
Doing one of his tornado twists,
Lunges forward with his flying fists,

And a gangster shrieks like a dinosaur,
Bodies all lying in a heap on the floor,
Now he's completed his life-long task,
Finally decides to remove his bright green mask,
Sensing her feelings are well on the wane,
How she misses her limelight and fame.
Fed up with falsehood and his persona,
Finds he's abandoned, becomes a loner,
How this green mask has failed to deliver,
And then he throws it back into the river.

Rapper's Dance

Rapper Ben turns up in Levi jeans,
Way down yonder in New Orleans,
Starting to rave at a night club bar,
Seeks to become a celebrity star;
Make an impression all over the land,
Bowing down to the black musician's band,
Sings in a mic and he steps up the tone,
Blowing in trumpet and sliding trombone,
Dancing around to the rhythm and blues,
Moving and clicking his shiny black shoes,
Snapping his fingers and rolling his eyes,
Sweating and making the temperature rise;
Going all hep with his magical feet,
Tapping in time with the jazz band's beat,
Rolling around like a demon possessed,
Seeing his heart thump right out of his chest,
Under the bright scarlet flickering lights,
Jumps in the air and he's hitting the heights.
See that his onlookers are all in a trance,
Put in a spell by this rapper's wild dance.

Three Native American Dances

Rain Dance

Shaman questioned what the thunder said,
Spoken over skulls in land of dead,
Where the prairie's dusty, parched and dry,
Beneath a hazy never-ending sky,
Looked upon a grave Comanche tribe,
Filled with sense of dread he couldn't hide,
Watched the trembling heatwaves rise in air,
Heightened by the scorching sun's bright glare,
Down by dried-up riverbed at Eagle Crag,
There he started dancing, turned, zigzagged,
All in rhythm to their drums that beat,
Cried out, moved around with stamping feet.
Worked up till he reached his depths of passion,
When the thunder boomed throughout the canyon,
Gazed above and saw a moving cloud,
Rolled across the heavens like a shroud,
Streaks of lightning put him in a trance,
Found he's wet through in this raving rain dance.

Hunter's Dance

He curses ravens circling Yellow Crag,
Sets a rapid pace in hunter's dance,
Shaman wears the antlers of a stag,
Thumping his feet with a side look glance.
Moves between the feathered flashing spears,
There in morning's rising round red sun.
Now he chants a theme from down the years,

Wakes departed spirits in age-old lands,
Shoots his bloodied arrows from his bow,
There among the firelit painted wigwams,
Sees his young braves' faces all aglow,
And he signals for the hunt to start,
Now he's fired them up within each heart.

War Dance

Drummer's fingers, tapping out the war dance beat,
Shaman vows to bring about white man's doom,
Sees his braves all move around with frenzied feet,
And a howling wolf beneath a bright full moon.
Then he summons spirits, where no vultures fly,
Somehow sends the frantic dancers in a trance,
Hears them yelling under starling starlit sky,
Leads his angry tribesmen in a warlike dance,
Then he summons spooks out from an ancient forest,
Shrunken skulls all stare and scream from round his belt.
Now he's filled with power and beats upon his breast,
Flinging out his hands, displays a white man's scalp,
Shakes his rattle and it makes his spirit soar,
Sees the weird faces in the bonfire's flames,
Hears the mountain and the river phantoms roar,
Enters region where the darkest terror reigns,
Whipping up his tribe, puts fire inside their souls,
How his wondrous magic rules the trembling air,
Makes those eyes all glare from eerie totem poles,
How it thrills the crazy shaman, Running Bear.

Mechanical Doll

He springs into life with a turn of a key,
Mechanical doll is so full of glee,
Dressed in a purple-and-yellow striped suit,
Fluttering his eyelashes and looking so cute,
Watches the blonde and the way she walks,
Seeing his eyes, when they pop out like stalks,
Dances to left and he dances to right,
Have you seen such a comical sight?
Tapping his feet on the nightclub bar,
Rising to status of a celebrity star,
Rapidly moves in his shiny black shoes,
Slowing right down to the rhythm and blues,
Pausing a moment to sip his champagne,
Starts off again like a man insane,
Goes up the wall and on to the ceiling,
Upside down and he's rocking and reeling,
Coming straight down and he touches the floor,
Pleased that the people erupt in a roar,
To the delight of this laughing clown,
Finds he's gradually winding down,
Ending his dance with a skip and a hop,
Comes to a stop and he falls with a flop!

Swan Lake

Grand celebrations in castle grounds,
Set on the countryside's highest mounds,
Kindly prince summons the poor to his party,
Jugglers and jokers and crooks and the crafty,
Beggars and blind men and even the lame,
Join in and feast on hog roast and rich game,
Drink from their huge frothy tankards of ale,
How he laughs when they rant and rail.
Now he's full of high spirits and fun,
Listens to musicians' flutes and a drum,
Watching the peasant girls dance with such flare,
Swishing their skirts in the trembling night air,
Moving around with their dancing feet,
Passions ablaze like the bonfire's red heat.
Mother's words haunt him from the castle hall,
'Find a bride at the coming court ball.'
Lively wild party now draws to a close,
Prince walks around and he sniffs a red rose,
Hears some swans' wings that are beating above,
That stirs his warm heart with desire and love.

Moonlight ripples on mountain's deep lake,
Graceful white swans leave their glistening wake,
Prince sees the swans turn to glorious girls,
Smiling white faces and flowing black curls.
Choosing one girl with a beautiful soul,
Moment when showers from the shooting stars roll,
Northern Lights with their innocent green,

Shining down onto his pure white Swan Queen,
Standing there in a gorgeous white gown,
Lovely figure with a bosom so round,
Finding her gentle, so soft and ethereal,
Overwhelmed that he meets his ideal,
Face his precious, beloved Odette.
Dancing so elegantly, moving in step,
Ballerina's poise and she's graceful and slow,
Spinning around like a top, on tiptoe,
Turns to her side and she's full of zest,
Leans right forward to an arabesque.
Springs to the left and then swings to the right,
Leaping up to tremendous height,
Moving so rapidly, there on her feet,
Sees her fall down on the ground in a heap;
Then she changes to swan in the dawn,
Midnight, turns back to her human form,
Under a magician's evil spell,
Cast from the edge of a darkening dell.
Magic now falls on the castle court ball,
Classical paintings light up on each wall,
Aristocrats, every one wearing a mask,
Elegant manner, that touch of class,
Chandeliers hang from a ceiling above,
Prince looks down and he picks up a glove.
Meeting the magician's daughter, Odile,
Find she bewitches him with a sweet smile,
Wearing some feathers just like a black swan,
Memories of Odette are now leading him on.
Raven hair falls on her heaving breast,
Piercing dark eyes, this mysterious guest,

Stepping forward, he kisses her hand,
Puts on silk glove and together they stand,
Slain by her passion, alluring dark charms,
And he surrenders into her arms.
Loves the orchestra sounding supreme,
Waltzing around in a wonderful dream,
Feeling his soul and his spirit soar,
Moving so swiftly across the stone floor,
Cultured movements look so refined,
Enter the heights of idolatrous mind,
Blind to Odette, who now pleads at the window,
There all in vain, with her heart filled with woe.
Now he reaches that place of pride,
Promises Odile will now be his bride.
Stunned, the hall is now plunged into darkness,
Sad he's become so completely heartless,
Highest rank proves to be no exception,
Now he's succumbed to the snare of deception.

Full of remorse with his heart full of grief,
Comes to the lake and he finds no relief,
Meeting his Odette with the swan maidens,
Asks for forgiveness and makes amends.
Sees she's distraught that he's bound by an oath,
Filled with woe that he's still betrothed,
Touched she hugs him and then jumps in the lake,
Follows her and thinks that his heart will break
And he forfeits all his position and wealth,
More than willing to sacrifice all self,
Suddenly finds that the spell is lifted,
Glad the black magician's power is dead.

Couple awake and they're feeling reborn,
Springing alive on this sunlit morn,
Running straight through the flowery green meadows,
Follow their spirit wherever it flows,
Under the fading pale moon's last quarter,
Seeing the stately white swans on the water,
Memories mirrored in the mountain's lake,
Certain and knowing which path to take,
They're unrestrained from the realms of time,
Now the eternal embraces divine.
Waterfall's power keeps on hammering,
Echoing, making the valleys all sing,
Lovers lie by an emerald-green pool,
That is now glittering like a jewel,
They both look up to those laughing rills,
Hearing a shepherd's song from the old hills,
Deeply in love and so happy together,
Here in a kingdom that lasts forever.

The Rapper

Now I'm well known as Jack the Lad,
Greatest young rapper that Ely has had,
And all my followers love to hear
Me broadcast from Radio Cambridgeshire.
Listen, I want you to understand,
I hold this city in palm of my hand,
Now I'm not all of what I seem,
Catching my drift if you know what I mean,
All the people who meet me step aside,
Do they realise I'm a Jekyll and Hyde?
When I speak through my microphone,
Find that I live in a world of my own.
I'm sophisticated, doffing my top hat,
Swinging my swagger stick, how about that?
Lapping up cheers from a gathering crowd,
Puffing me up and making me proud,
Some people think I'm a bit of a toff,
A scallywag and a great big show-off.
See how my energy springs into life,
When I'm involved in some drama or strife,
The other extreme, oh, my giddy aunt!
Cathedral choir when they're singing plainchant,
Overcome by its beauty and charm,
Make my hairs stand on the back of my arm,
Obsessive to an extreme degree,
Up in the clouds when I'm really free.
Here in this nightclub, I prop up the bar,
Claiming the fame of a celebrity star,

Dancing around to the rhythm and blues,
How can I live up to all this ruse?
When my thoughts all race out of control,
I'm worried about the state of my soul,
Know what happens when I take off my mask,
Whatever comes next, will you please not ask,
There are times when I sit and brood,
Completely drained, in an awful mood.
Later I'm faced with a sense of doom,
Covered in a cloak of darkness and gloom,
A visit from my vicious black dog,
Grovelling in mud and I'm low as a hog,
Those sneering grim faces that mock me from Hell,
I'm gripped and I'm trapped in this dreadful spell,
My eyes transfixed in a ghostly stare,
Yet I find my release through the power of prayer.

Places and Events

Fingal's Cave

Lonely Scottish Isle in Hebrides,
Where a giant cathedral cave delights,
Sea breathes music through its holy sanctuary,
Grandeur from its lofty organ pipes,
Thunder in mighty breakers of the ocean,
Beating like fury on that rocky shore,
Setting darkening, rolling clouds in motion,
Fills those wrestling white-capped waves with awe,
Makes those ancient Celtic gods all sing,
Spellbound and appear in their mystical past,
Stirs those restless heavens with forked lightning,
Leaves seafaring phantom sailors aghast;
Never ceasing to hum their haunting tune,
There beneath a mellow midnight moon.

The Cruel Sea

The Kingdom of the Sea's silver capped breakers
Crash on the ancient Celtic cliffs in Cornwall,
Are driven by a strong south-westerly breeze,
And develop into a full-blown squall.
She welcomes a sailing ship from the past,
Sees it wrestle with whistling wind and wave,
Its ghostly sailors beneath a reeling mast,
All stare in terror at her watery grave;
Still fighting with her never-ending fury,
She feels them toss and turn in her merciless womb,
Amused their ebbing spirits are growing weary,
Wait for them to sink in her bottomless tomb.

She watches them rising up to her dizzy heights,
And being sucked into her whirring whirlpool,
Shaking when a flash of lightning strikes,
She spins their ship around and acts so cruel;
Furious with the helmsman at the wheel,
Skilfully escapes the cursed ship's fate,
When he and his crew renew their zeal,
That increases her bitterness and hate.
She knows that all their efforts will be in vain,
As they hear her voice cry from the deep,
Clearly in spite of the wind and pouring rain,
'Come and join me in my endless sleep.'

Then she forces the wounded ship to a bay,
Spitting out her foam like a witch's broth,

Mocking the crippled crew along their way,
And shows them the fullness of her wroth,
There beneath a thunderbolt's echoing boom,
She laughs at them vibrate from electric shocks,
Sees the men, who finally meet their doom,
Perish among the hidden razor-sharp rocks.
How she glories and revels in the hubbub,
With bodies scattered on the broken deck,
She's alarmed when she's turning into blood,
Surrounds those pieces of floating ship wreck.
Now bloodied, she rears up and starts to gawp,
When stars are falling like golden tears,
Finding she enters into a time warp,
And surprised when a glowing red moon appears,
Now she's aware her kingdom has come to an end,
And her waves will no longer seethe or roar,
When the cruel sea dries up in every land,
She'll not sound upon the shore anymore.

Demonic Storm

Down in a village on the coast of Cornwall,
Sounds the chilling, chiming church's bell,
Wild north-west wind whistles on its way,
Wobbling all the ships in that restless bay,
Threatening swirling dark clouds fill the sky,
Thunder flashes, fork lightning on high,
Driving rain strikes the window panes,
Running down those pipes into drains,
Fishermen's cottages are gripped with fear,
They see a gang of ghostly pirates appear.
Water dripping down like sweat from ceilings,
Everybody's haunted with macabre feelings,
Alarmed by the banging on the roofs,
Streets echo with clopping cloven hoofs,
They see them gather into a great throng,
Dance the sailors' hornpipe and sing a song.
Ill gusts of wind, winch open the door,
And stench of seaweed shakes them to the core,
That phantom pirate ship, seen from the quay,
With its anchor fastened, far out to sea.
Somehow, they find themselves there on board,
Terrified by the ghostly crew who roared,
And skeleton pirates on reeling mast,
Hear their bones all rattling in stormy blast,
Feel the ship sink down onto seabed,
Here they come to dark realms of the dead;
Then swallowed up into the depths of Hell,
Greeted by creatures and fiends so foul,

They sail on through a sea of fire,
And sea shanties sung by a demonic choir,
As the ship goes down in a whirlpool,
Taunted by every devil and ghoul,
As it spirals further and further down,
On to an endless journey underground,
They come to a wonderland of ice,
Shiver in this place of paradise,
Sparkle with every kind of precious gem,
Devil's cloak glitters, right down to the hem.
They hear beating wings of an albatross,
Their thoughts all turn to the Christian cross,
When they awake from this bad nightmare,
They welcome the rising sun and salty sea air.

Medieval Fayre

Ely Cathedral stands like a ship on a hill,
Floating on the flowery bright green meadows,
Some haunting monks' ancient voices thrill
The soul with their Latin plainchant that flows
In praise beneath the glorious Fenland skies,
Trembling like tongues of fire in springtime air,
Moving a pretty girl chasing butterflies,
There on her way to a medieval fayre.

The Morris dancers' ankle bells all ring,
Stirring the locals with their foursome reels,
Evoking spirits peeping from a spring,
Harlequins spin around like Catherine wheels,
Happy minstrels singing and plucking their harps,
Falconer's hawk seizes its prey on high,
Punch and Judy creating gasps and laughs
And children not knowing whether to scream or cry.

Some comical clowns all prance in procession,
Red lips, painted faces as pale as a ghost,
Mingle with the merry peasants and yeomen,
Teasing fat friars gorging the hog roast;
Guzzling from their frothy tankards of mead,
Finding themselves stumbling and lost in a maze,
Suffering from their gluttony and their greed,
Meet the twin-horned Devil all ablaze.

A crowd falls under a dramatic poet's spell,
Words spoken from a biblical mystery play,
Watching a dragon rise from the flames of Hell,
Christ the Saviour appears and bars his way;
Sends an angel to hurl him into the abyss,
Chained in a dungeon for a thousand years,
Swishing his tail in anger with a hiss,
Deep in darkness, where he snarls and sneers.

Jesters larking around and cracking jokes,
Upset some witches from the same coven,
And they ride on their bearded nanny goats,
Hope they won't be baked inside their oven.
A young fire-eater breathing out his flames,
Before a bubbly, big, black-breasted bear,
The people elated from these fun and games,
Rave here at this medieval fayre.

Hilton Maze

A traveller hurried down a shady lane,
Through picturesque Hilton village,
Chased by a fiend that proved to be a bane,
Plagued him on this road to pilgrimage,
He could feel his burning brimstone breath;
As he crossed a rippling ford,
Haunted by his clopping hoofs of death,
Terror pierced his heart like a sword.

He came to the turf-green maze just in time,
Ran in circles to its centre,
Knew evil only moves in a straight line,
Relieved this devil couldn't enter.
He stood before his pair of shining horns,
Fear soon gripped him from within,
Waited there, disturbed by his gathering fauns,
How he hated his sarcastic grin.

Later he watched him under the evening sun,
Summon a host of cackling elves,
Mischievous and so bent on poking fun,
It troubled him how they excelled themselves,
When he heard those windows and doors all slam
In the village, where children screamed,
Flying saucepans and kettles made such a clang,
He sensed how it pleased that wicked fiend.

At night he saw the witches sweeping their broomsticks
In widdershins, dark evil flow,
And it almost scared him out of his wits,
Beneath the sickle-shaped moon aglow,
Seemed to reap the stars from their bed,
When flames of fire licked round the maze,
Scores of spirits visited him from the dead,
While the devil laughed in the blaze.

Knapwell Wood

How young Sylvia loved this month of May,
Sunlight sparkled on her auburn hair,
Such a sweet aroma followed her,
As her footsteps glided through the air,
On a well-worn path to Knapwell Wood,
Where chestnuts trees and blossom adorned hedgerows,
Further on, she came to a church that stood
On a slope overlooking some meadows,
She caught a glimpse of an old thatched cottage,
Then entered a sunlit rounded archway of green,
Soon her feet thumped on a wooden bridge,
There she gazed into a weaving stream.
She loved the stillness between the woodland trees,
Imagined those feet that trod its ancient paths,
Then caught a whiff from the springtime breeze,
Cheered along by a couple of chiffchaffs,
Where water bubbled in some springs and wells,
She heard a woodpecker drilling in the bark,
Then bowed before a beautiful bed of bluebells,
And its fragrance wafted and touched her heart.
She loved the joy that lived in every hue,
Bees hummed in harmony round wild honeysuckle,
The frequent low notes from the merry cuckoo,
And deep down she felt her belly chuckle.
She stared between the majestic English elms,
Like feelings stirred inside a holy place,
After she wandered beyond nature's realms
And found eternity stared her in the face.

She's shocked to see a vision beyond the grave,
A moated manor house, Overhall Grove,
Even voices from a banquet raved,
And seemed to haunt her, wherever she roved.
She stood and stared a while before her host,
Admired her blue and scarlet ankle-length gown,
Spellbound by the features of this ghost,
Her dark hair rested on her bosom so round,
She watched her slender fingers plucking her lyre,
Carried away by her high soprano voice,
Played havoc and touched her deepest desire,
That seemed to make the whole of nature rejoice,
Surprised this music rose to such a height,
Until she felt herself all filled with love,
And soared like the wings of a red kite,
She heard it blend with angels singing above.

She's overcome by heat on this lazy afternoon,
When the eye of heaven shone too hot,
And those blithe birds sung a softer tune,
When the church clock's hands reached three o'clock,
She laid among the sweet, cool blades of grass,
And felt weary and decided to take a nap,
After a while she drifted into the past,
With a daisy chain nestled on her lap.
She dreamt about a gnarled ancient grey oak,
With white-hooded Druids gathered round,
Listened to them reciting their rhymes by rote,
Then she found her heart began to pound,
Later on, she woke up with a start,
She stretched her arms, yawned, and still in a daze,

In a dream so vivid that she's taken part,
Still haunted by those Beltane fires ablaze.
The mottled scarlet skies seem to brood,
Its atmosphere made her more intense,
Captivated by this strange enchanting mood,
Found she's moved by the flowers rising incense,
Enhanced by the birds' mystical sea of song,
All its depth of feeling and here she'll abide,
And carried on its wave, she drifted along
In those magical moments at eventide.

Nightfall had put on its dark black hood,
Short-eared bats all darted to and fro,
She made her way down into Knapwell Wood,
Her lantern light from the moon's bright glow.
She heard high-pitched notes from a nightingale,
Her spirit lifted by this sweet serenade,
Underneath the stars in their silvery veil,
And relieved her fears began to fade.
The middle of the wood seemed rather dark,
Where her mind imagined all sorts of things,
This soon followed by a sudden spark,
She faced a host of fairies' golden wings,
It seemed like somebody had struck a match,
That lit up a springtime elfin carnival.
She's horrified she's stepped right into their patch,
Among this hive of activity down in the dell,
She found herself mingling with the crowd,
Marvelled how an elfin king looked so merry,
There by his side, even more than proud,
A queen with puffed up cheeks, red as a cherry,

A joker's bells rung on his three-cornered hat,
Fire-eater breathed out a stream of flames,
Harlequin behaved like an accomplished acrobat,
There performed his tricks and funny games.
Inside the palace garden she saw a maid,
On a toadstool, peddling a spinning wheel,
The yarn sparkled like her golden braid,
And its magic rhythm filled her with zeal,
She joined with fairies and elves in a lively dance,
And she reached such a pitch with her moving feet,
Mesmerised, then drawn into a dream-like trance,
Alarmed when she could hear her thumping heartbeat.

The vision vanished, she'd never felt such peace,
Like Benedictine nuns' voices at prime,
That sense of power about to be released,
When a few piping birds would touch the sublime,
Inspire the rest to erupt in a rapturous roar,
And their musical notes travelled everywhere,
Overwhelmed and it made her spirit soar,
As she absorbed its joy that filled the air,
It sounded like a full-blown orchestra,
How she revelled in this celestial choir,
Echoed beneath the bright and morning star,
She embraced the glorious glow from its fire.
She bid her farewell to a fading moon,
Between the trees, she welcomed a giant red orb,
That defied the darkness, rose forth from its tomb,
She felt its strength as it moved further forward,
Clothed in a majestic purple-coloured robe,
She marvelled when nature's energy came alive,

Lit from its great gigantic golden globe,
Captured that moment when heaven and earth revive,
In this happy season, when spring's reborn,
At a time when everything felt so good,
Although she realised another day would dawn,
She'd never forget her visit to Knapwell Wood.

The Battle of the Somme

Our troops think the Huns flashing guns never tire,
With its shells whistling on through a grey sky,
Rhythmic rattle from machine gunfire,
Rat-a tat-tat, you are going to die.
Singing its song in the battle at Somme,
Rings in the ears of the anxious young tommies,
Nursing their anger and woe for so long,
Its melody haunting and torturing their memories.
When their young officer's whistle blows,
Soldiers all scramble out of their trenches,
Will they come back? Nobody knows,
Scuttling over the barbed-wire fences,
Their faces show up in the shellfire's flare,
Spurred on by those Scottish bagpipes,
Hear aeroplanes that are humming in the air,
The terrifying din from their droning dogfights.
They've come to a place to face their worst fears,
Stifling smoke from an exploding shell,
And their cheeks are now running with tears,
Tormented in these darkest depths of hell,
Caught in the brunt of the enemy's attack,
Running forward with their leaden feet,
Finding everywhere going pitch black,
And they no longer hear their heartbeat.

Rumbling guns fade to an eerie silence,
Bare black tree branches fill this landscape,
Moving white mists make the scene more intense,

This graveyard where all the men meet their fate,
Their body parts are now sown in mud,
Phantoms move over the sodden field,
Dark Angel's scythe is dripping with blood,
Reaping dark death as its daily yield,
Stands there triumphant on a hill,
Mocking the plight of these valiant men,
In no man's land, now so lifeless and still,
Surely the nation will remember them.

Soham Station Disaster

Steam train approaches the station of Soham,
Coming along on a single-track line,
Fifty-one wagons all creak and groan,
Darkness and fate are a matter of time.
Train now seems that it's barely awake,
Engine is sweating with tension and fear,
Making the dragging long-wagons shake,
Chugging through fenlands and haunted mere,
Sluggish and slowest of munitions trains,
Puffing and panting and all out of breath,
Leading wagon now bursts into flames,
Dicing around with the demons of death,
Threatening chaos on sleeping town,
On this sweltering hot night in June,
Most of its people are bedded down,
There in the light of a silvery moon.
Driver and fireman are filled with terror,
Bringing the train to a grinding halt,
Fireman uncouples the blazing wagon,
Jumps back on train and moves off with a jolt;
Speeding away with its flammable load
And like sheet lightning it lights up the sky,
As the bombs in the wagon explode!
Both the fireman and signalman die:
There in a crater that's sixty-feet wide,
Lie in a grave that is fifteen-feet deep,
Angel of Death with his sweeping scythe,
Laughs at the people disturbed from their sleep.

Four brave men saved the town from destruction,
Its inhabitants from the full force of the blast,
Here on that night at this railway station,
They'll be remembered in years that pass.

The Fox Hunt

See those galloping huntsmen awake the red dawn,
Right behind those bloodthirsty and barking wild hounds,
With that sound from the riders and hunter's brass horn
And their thunderous hoofs in a mansion's huge grounds,
The imaginary military charge on the ha-ha,
And eventually reaching Old Raven Hall chase,
With their horses pounding the earth with a jar,
And they're going along at a terrific pace,
The young horsemen all feeling a bracing cool breeze,
So uplifting it gives them a superior air,
And they're thrilled by the ritual black rooks in the trees,
This is bringing alive, all their upper-class flare,
There right under the morning skies blazing dark red,
And they pass and they startle a bull and his cows,
They're all chasing the hounds that are racing ahead
And they're jumping hedges with sweat on their brows,
As they're gathering speed in a flowery green meadow,
Through the woodlands and straight over the ditches and dykes,
And their splashing in streams with their cheeks all aglow,
Now their spirits all reach their heroic grand heights.
They're all filled with bloodlust on the crest of a hill,
See that cornered red fox that is all out of breath,
As their ravenous hounds go in for their kill,
And the fox's life ends with a horrific death.

Trampoline

Young child jumps up on a trampoline,
Here on a lawn in a garden so green,
Whizzing around in a somersault,
Going straight up in the heaven's blue vault,
Bursting with energy, purpose in life,
Without a care and with freedom from strife,
Bouncing high up and then down like a spring,
Soaring like a young bird on the wing,
Every slick movement so full of fine fun,
In the sight of the smiling gold sun,
Hitting the heights with much joy and laughter,
Young child lives happily ever after,
Clearly expressed in his hype and his power,
That captures eternity within an hour.

Psyche and Cupid

Crashing waves all hissing round the rocks,
Beautiful figure rises from white sea foam,
Goddess of love with falling golden locks,
There she stands on a pearly seashell throne.
White-winged Cupid with bow and arrow,
Its sharp head tipped with passion and desire,
Flying straighter, swifter than a sparrow,
There over a sparkling sea of sapphire.
How she triumphs when it finds its mark,
Stirring restlessness within the soul,
Overwhelming pleasure pierces a wounded heart,
Leaving it with a glorious sense of the whole,
When fiery passion reigns and flows so free,
That is heightened by the spirit of Psyche.

Jack Frost

Jack Frost brings dark winter's gloom,
Chilling that cobbled Cotswold street,
Sparkling beneath a silvery moon,
There he offers his seasonal treat.
Then he comes to market square,
Stands beside a Christmas tree,
Shining in the cold and crispy air,
That now fills his heart with glee.

When that evening sun goes down,
Watches a herd of running deer,
Proudly wears his holly crown,
Here in this festive time of year.
How he loves the country landscape,
Breathes and freezes 'friar's pond,'
Teaches the local children to skate,
And he takes their dreams beyond.
Then he glitters on the graves,
Loves to hear the choirboys sing,
Finds that his Christmas spirit raves,
Now the chiming church bells ring.
Then he stands so high on a hill,
Jumps onto a children's sledge,
Sliding so fast it gives him a thrill,
But he finishes up in a hedge.

When he comes to Tudor Hall,
Icicles form a freezing fountain,

Laughing now the snowflakes fall,
And delighted, he covers the garden.
Later, he teases a hireling shepherd,
Pleased how he shivers with cold,
Melting ice drips down his beard,
Then he drives his sheep in the fold.
After a while, he wallows in power,
Under the skies all red and mauve,
He's cut off each leaf and flower,
Birds no longer sing in the grove.
There he drinks in Queen of Hearts,
Under hanging mistletoe,
Where he kisses a pretty maiden,
Then he hears a watery flow.
Frantic, he bursts in those depths of night,
Where he finds his fatal flaw,
Underneath the sparkling starlight,
There he starts to run and thaw.

A Spring Garden

Spring, and I rise from slumber with a yawn,
Shafts of sunlight streaming through my bedroom
Window, hear those songbirds praising the dawn,
As I gaze on my garden in full bloom.
Wearily I tread the spiral stair,
Swing open my solid oak cottage door,
Breathing in the cool, fresh, fragrant air,
Wish this moment would last for evermore,
Watching my swathe of golden daffodils,
Trumpet in this glorious stately spring.
Deep blue hyacinths scent my windowsills,
Yellow hammers whistling on the wing,
Waters moving in a babbling brook,
Spread of violets sunning in their bed,
Lady smock nearby a shady nook,
Skylarks trilling high overhead.
Summer's coming, bees are humming,
Swarming, buzzing round my purple lilac,
Faraway I hear a woodpecker drumming,
Golden-eyed cowslips crown a hillock;
Then I'm enchanted by a nightingale,
Love its warbling clear and tuneful notes,
Pierce this place where peace and joy prevail,
With its melody and fuels my hopes
And dreams, become the happiest of men,
See eternal present in every flower,
Harmony reigns within my spring garden,
And I feel its beauty pulsate with life and power.

Flaming June

A walk through the countryside in flaming June,
See how its grandeur fills those clear blue skies,
And that lazy cuckoo hurries his tune,
Where meadows teem with ladylike butterflies,
With bees all humming round the honeysuckle,
They pause a moment, hear when summer sings,
Even the restless sparrows dart and chuckle,
There above, a high hawk spreads his wings.
When the shimmering hot day comes to a close,
And those evening shadows start to fall,
Highlights a scented old-fashioned rose,
Flourishes by a mansion's garden wall,
Some purple clouds now bubble overhead,
Underneath the glowing sun's round red disc,
The flowers all smiling sweetly from their bed,
Hark how birdsong blesses this glorious bliss.

July

What pleasure, during this month of hot July,
Its sky all painted in vivid blue so clear,
To feel the glowing sun's roving eye.

All seeing, bringing clarity of a seer,
Brightens a quaint whitewashed, thatched cottage,
With memories overflowing, with moments held dear.

Those cawing rooks in chestnut trees at the vicarage,
Red fuchsias' lanterns on either side of a lawn,
With its lily pond and hump-stone bridge,

And far in the distance, hear a hunter's horn,
With maidens in meadows wearing summer frocks,
Gaze at the poppies, swaying in golden corn,

Go back to their garden, by the glaring hollyhocks,
In the evening shadow's warm embrace,
Then capture a whiff from the night-scented stocks.

Under a glimpse from the sun's round red face,
With the pink and purple skies all ablaze,
Will all soon disappear without a trace.

Yet it will never cease to please or amaze.

Mystical Wales

The Aber waterfall with its long white train,
Majestic as a ghostly Celtic king,
We feel his presence through his timeless reign,
Find it touches us through the depths of our being,
As surging waters hammer in our brain,
Slithering on their way, weaving between
The grey rocks, under the sunlit golden boughs,
We admire their wealth of leaves so green,
And hear the sound of rhythmic waters arouse
A dark and beautiful sleepless Celtic queen.

A weary summer sun reaches its lowest phase,
Darkens the ever-rocky river that roars,
We gaze at the evening skies all red with rage,
Catch a glimpse from Welsh red dragon's claws,
We're mesmerised by its yellow eyes ablaze.
We watch it rise, flapping its wings in flight,
Casting its shadow over mountains and hills,
How its living streams of fire delight,
Its grandeur glowing in the valleys and rills,
We're all overcome by this glorious sight.

We travel through Horseshoe Pass at Llangollen,
And join the people at the Eisteddfod,
Chanting a poem on the magical Celtic cauldron,
The harp strings plucked by raven-haired Ingrid,
Then followed by the antlered Morris men;
Their folk dance takes us way back down the years,

Imagine we're among a circle of standing stones,
And captivated by its haunting atmosphere,
The power flows from this area of cosmic thrones,
We feel an empathy with its Druidic seers.

Political and
Religious Poems

Great Britain's Brexit

The pride of Great Britain, the Houses of Parliament,
Have now come to a time when daylight ends,
With the going down of a red sunset,
That wavers on the serpentine River Thames.
A shadow of darkness falls over Westminster,
Where the princes and powers of the air all prey
Around, spreading out their leathery sinister
Black wings, they whisper, 'Europe's the only path',
Parade their propaganda without pity,
Chanting their motto, 'Many tongues, one voice',
Echo across the great bard's unreal city,
Now prepares the path for the Antichrist.

The politicians cackling like a parliament of fowls,
Frustrate the nation for three-and-a-half years,
The spiritual forces elude these wise old owls,
That puts the people through blood, sweat and tears;
Like a ship that's caught in a whirring whirlpool,
Forever spinning round, round and round,
And they're still under Europe's defiant rule,
They seem to be going over the same old ground.
What will it take to break through this impasse?
With Boris seeking to find a new solution,
Equipped with the finest touch of Etonian class,
And bring a final halt to this revolution.
A couple of traitors hire a high court judge,
Under the influence of a revived Roman empire,
Encourage the government's taste for further fudge,

Then plunging themselves deeper into the mire,
Actually, having the nerve to make Brexit illegal,
Attempting to rob our nation of its will,
Rising over the public like an eagle,
Never seem satisfied of having their fill.
This is hardly the time for people to rejoice,
Hark, Margaret Thatcher screams from her grave,
And repeats, 'Listen to the people's voice',
This lady's not for turning, please behave.
Take a leaf out of the book from Henry the Eighth,
He had the courage to sever ties from Rome,
And put Britain on a path to become great,
With its fine architecture, all set in stone.
Now enter the Machiavellian red dragon,
Descending straight down a bottomless gorge,
Landing in the fires of Hell to his den,
All blazing fiercer than a blacksmith's forge,
Terrified voices among the spitting sparks,
With shining gold in a magic forest fire,
Constantly torments the Satanist Karl Marx,
His fate for carrying out the Devil's desire,
Influencing politicians to peddle a pack of lies,
Using sophistry like Mephistopheles,
Made to look like virtue in many eyes,
With paupers ruling the princes, is disease.
How about the refreshing jolly joker?
With a bright, broad grin from ear to ear,
Encourages Trump to bluff in a game of poker,
And singing this song between his sips of beer.
'When they were in, they were in,
When they were out, they were out,

When they were only halfway in,
They were neither in or out.'
A crowd of puppets headed by Canterbury,
Deceived by a melody from Babylon,
And they're in the same old boat all merry,
Rolling along singing a rousing song,
Liberal, left-wing and some into multi-faith,
Chanting all together in a sweet refrain,
Counter-reformation stares like a wraith,
They repeat their chorus, 'Remain, remain, remain'.
Secular humanism blocks our heritage and culture,
Allies itself with the grim black master of death,
Preying and circling like a hungry vulture,
It devours flesh till only bare bones are left.
They make a lousy job of playing God,
Leading the nation into a Satanic snare,
Having people walking around like zombies,
They unaware the demonic realm is out there.
Boris's Brexit should start with chiming Big Ben,
This symbolic sound remembered over the years,
Revive Britain's heartbeat all over again,
Moving the nation forward, side-stepping fears,
When at last, Europe's dictatorship now ends,
With our British government reigning supreme,
A wheel of fireworks lights up the River Thames,
While a band is playing 'God save the Queen'.
The nation moves from death to resurrection of power,
Marching onwards with sword of the spirit in hand,
Embrace our sovereignty in this triumphant hour,
Forever in England's green and pleasant land.

Rule, Britannia!

Europe's anchor holds our ship at bay,
Some of its squabbling sailors refuse to sail,
Captain Boris must shout 'Anchor aweigh!'
Come what wind, what may, rough sea or gale;
Time and tide, is right to bid farewell,
To arrogant Europe's control and blackmail.
Fire a cannonball straight across its bow,
And hear its gathering demons rant and rail.
Remainers raving at the port in uproar,
Whipping up bitter winds and waves so harsh,
Like sirens screaming from Britannia's shore,
The ship's departure leaves them all aghast.
'Rule, Britannia! Britannia, rule the waves!
Britons never, never, never shall be slaves.'

Weather forecast: cloudy, sunny and fair,
Trumpet calling from across the pond,
Deutschland all at sea and up in the air,
The Mayflower faces that fiend that lurks beyond;
Waiting, preying, like a giant red squid,
Threatening to swallow our nation whole,
Propaganda, who's he trying to kid?
Stealer of the younger generation's soul;
Marxism seeks to steer her ship off course,
Creates havoc in a raging storm,
We're all aware it takes nations by force,
And you'll never find a darker red dawn.
'Rule, Britannia! Britannia, rule the waves!

Britons never, never, never shall be slaves.'

Left has shipwrecked Christians on an island,
Brainwashing the nation with their liberal fog,
Hides Christian treasure from everyday man,
Pirates all filled with power and playing God.
Don't they realise what made this nation great?
Their sophistry just like a dead man's bones,
Pawn their prejudice with hearts so full of hate,
Ultimately comes from those demonic zones.
Spin doctors weave their evil web,
Severe with faces like a hat of crabs,
Don't do God and more in league with the dead,
Give the common man the screaming abdabs.
Then there's the professor inside his garden
Tending his evolutionary gem,
Not giving a thought to a perishing world,
Has he considered the New Jerusalem?
Colleges now seek to ban *The Daily Mail*,
Seem to be under the hammer and sickle,
Revel in power as it spreads through the nation,
Surely gets everyone in a hell of a pickle.
BBC, now in ship's dark hold,
Clapped in Marx and Engels' rusty chains,
Blinker their vision and left out in the cold,
This is what happens when Marxism reigns.
Now when a Christian's brought before court,
Law now seems to be that black is white,
But whoever would think in a modern world,
They'd attempt to snuff out Britannia's light.
'Rule, Britannia! Britannia, rule the waves!

Britons never, never, never shall be slaves.'

The time has come to break that Roman yoke,
Legions once marched right through London,
Fought until the British will be broke,
Cruelty to Christians in the Colosseum,
Surpassed only by that Tower of Babel,
Many tongues one voice from Babylon,
Captain Boris will keep Great Britain stable,
Join all together and sing this joyful song.
'Rule, Britannia! Britannia, rule the waves!
Britons never, never, never shall be slaves.'

European Union

In Strasbourg stands that proud tall Tower of Babel,
With its slogan, 'Many tongues, one voice',
Haunting its Roman-styled colosseum,
Hear the spirit of the Antichrist rejoice.
Christians, like human torches, blazing with fire,
Light up Emperor Nero's chariot races,
Crowds' passions that seem to be so dire,
Stare with ghoulish looks upon their faces.
The sheer cruelty doesn't make them weary,
Working up their appetites for more,
Whips them up into a demonic fury.
The tension erupts with an almighty roar;
When raging waters flood the whole arena,
They mock the valiant Christian gladiators,
Clad in hides and skins of wild animals
And face those hungry, wild alligators.
Watched above by princes and powers of the air,
Breathing out their smoking brimstone breath,
There in the evening's red and purple skies,
Delight in the presence and that stench of death.
Europa mounts a bull with dazzling horns,
Shining in the power of a crescent moon,
She rides a beast on surging waves of the sea,
And on land she finally meets her doom.
Now Queen of Heaven, crowned in halo of stars,
Seeing her son's face glowing in the sunburst,
Shining, deceiving the Roman Catholic Church,
Receive that ancient Babylonian curse.

Scaffolding protruding on eastern side of tower,
Many facets of ancient and modern design,
Stating Europe is evolving and unfinished,
Express its motion through those realms in time;
With geometric, elliptical structures,
That all is welcome through that Ishtar Gate,
Nations gripped by its democratic power,
And one day will form into a superstate.
The warning of clay all mixed with cast-iron feet,
With its political, religious and cultural mix,
Wait for him to sit in Satan's seat,
His son's number is 666!

Four Horsemen of the Apocalypse

Conquer comes between those parting clouds,
Riding on his large white horse,
He wears a crown and holds a golden bow,
To overcome the earth by force;
Prepares the way for the coming battlefield,
For every tribe, tongue and nation will yield.

Hoof beats shake those closing doors of sunset,
A horse appears that's fiery red,
Like that moon, with stars all falling like spears,
War now fills the earth with dread;
Glad that fighting is raging for all it's worth,
Now peace is taken away around the earth.

Out from the depths of darkness, a horse, jet black,
With its coat mere skin and bone,
Trotting through cities, reeks of rotten flesh,
Where thousands of bodies lie and groan,
Earth is reeling, panting and out of breath,
It's sick of this misty graveyard so full of death.

Grim Reaper sweeps his gruesome scythe,
Astride a horse so deadly pale,
Leading a host of demons and horrors from Hell,
Time when the master of death will prevail;
Will herald that false prophet and the beast,
Highlight evil in this pagan feast.

The Seven Seals of Judgement

A dark rider sat on his white horse with a bow,
Bent on his conquest and received a victorious crown,
And he came from the red fiery cracked plains in Hell,
How he gloated about all his power and renown;
In a time when a sense of all hope will cease,
As his thundering hoof beats increased in pace,
On his mission to rob all the earth of its peace,
And it brought on much suffering to human race.

Then a rider appeared on a dazzling red horse,
And he plunged the whole world in a horrific war,
As he galloped and trampled on piles of the dead,
How those mushroom clouds made his spirit soar;
With this fearsome warrior, puffed up with pride,
And roused all those demons in flaming furnace,
And he strengthened and quickened his horse's stride,
And he passed black smoke billowing from the abyss.

Yet another dark rider sat on his jet-black horse,
And so thrilled at the passionate beating black heart
There in Hell, now that hunger has taken its course,
On that day when all dignity had to depart,
And he brought so much pain where his horse's hoofs trod,
Straight across a worn torn land that looked so grave,
Now that death had become just like a greedy hog,
How he laughed at the demons that ranted and raved.

Then a pale horse showed up, its rider named Death,
With those horrors of Hades now following him,
And his horse was now breathing his brimstone breath,
As this Devil delights in dark death with its sin,
And his number of legions that shook the ground,
And he gripped the whole world in his evil spell,
As he reveled in fear that was all around,
Now the whole world was under the auspices of Hell.

When the Saviour began to break open the fifth seal,
Saw slain souls there beneath the altar of God,
And were fueled with a justice all brimming with zeal,
And those martyrs all screamed to avenge their spilt blood.
When an earthquake that brought destruction and doom,
How it aged the old sun and it changed to sackcloth,
In the heavens at night, a bright red blood moon,
When the Lord God Almighty had showed his wroth,
And the shinning stars dropped like some figs from a tree,
Then the sky soon receded and rolled up like a scroll.
Moved the mountains and islands with nowhere to flee,
Like the kings and princes had taken its toll.
Now all human resistance had faded away,
When disaster rode on all over the land,
That completed the sixth seal on this Judgement Day,
In that time in the wrath of the Lamb, who can stand?

When the Saviour broke open the seventh seal,
There was silence in Heaven for half an hour,
When the seven grand angels were given trumpets,
In that moment when God showed his great power,
The saints' prayers and incense burned on an altar,

Put in censor of gold in an angel's hand,

Then he hurled it on earth and rumbled and thundered,

And it caused a giant earthquake throughout the parched land.

The Dragon Cast Down to Earth

High up in Heaven, appeared a wondrous sign,
Sun-clothed – a woman, with moon under her feet,
A crown of twelve stars on her head all shine.

Yet another sign that seeks to compete,
A seven-horned dragon with crowns like kings
On seven heads, he let out an angry shriek!

This giant red dragon beating his leathery wings,
He's furious being cast down upon the earth,
With his rebellious heart, harder than stone,

And annoyed when the woman gives birth,
Seeing her child snatched up to the throne in Heaven,
The dragon pursues her with all his worth,

Seething when God hides her in the desert,
Dragon leaves to fight a war in the heavenlies,
In an encounter between angels and demons,

And he and his principalities
And powers are hurled down to earth once again,
Are angered by the martyrs' testimonies,

All the dragon's evil passions are inflamed,
Spewing out torrents of a river in a fit,
To drown the fleeing woman, his only aim,

But saw God open the earth and swallow it,
He sees the woman escape and he's filled with fury,
And a sense of revenge now rules his spirit.

He crouches down on the shore by the sea,
And his son the beast comes out of the waves,
Welcomes the second in the counterfeit trinity,

The false prophet comes out the land and he raves,
When folks worship the beast's statue there
In the city square, by those mass graves,

Delights the master of death, this prince of the air,
That roaming hungry dragon, seeks to devour.

Harlot Rides the Beast

High above where a howling dark tempest raves,
Threatens a burning rough sea of white water and fire,
Hundreds of souls that are screaming beneath the waves,

Finding no rest in this furious funeral pyre,
Pouring out loads of their miseries on the shore,
Hissing among all those rattling grey stones in ire,

Deafened by a deep furnace that rumbles and roars,
Watching demonic horsemen ride out of the abyss
And they're tormented by an evil that now soars;

Winch at their lightning, wild whips in their midst,
Knowing these warriors of war will soon clearly excel,
Bring on death and destruction on all who resist.

Now they're haunted, enchanted by monastery bell,
Hear monks singing the Sanctus in plainchant and song,
Echo around all those cathedral caves in Hell;

Steeped in idolatry from the ancient Babylon,
Watching monks who are mourning in mass for the dead,
Seeing the satanic spirits all leading them on,

Walking along in procession and lantern-led,
Blinded by light that's coming straight from the sunburst,
Stare in those skies and surprised by a moon, blood red,

Worship the Queen of Heaven in spite of her curse,
Feeling the presence of something so foul, yet so grand,
Marvel at zodiac signs all aglow in the universe,
Meeting that red dragon that's stomping in desert sand,
Watching the harlot young queen who is riding this beast,
Drink from the sins from the gold cup in her hand.

They celebrate with those demons all at this feast,
Dazzled by her bright purple and scarlet cloak,
Just like the bishops in mitres, deceived as the priests;

Sharing the woe with this woman, beyond all hope,
Touched by her precious cut stones and her glittering gold,
Cheered by the blood of the saints and it makes them gloat,

Seeing her going astride in such pomp, yet so cold,
And the fuming dark hatred that glows from the dragon,
Moving around, they're amazed when she loses her hold,

And how this creature abhors all her false religion,
Devours her flesh and that burning of every bone,
Destroys the mother of harlots and mystery Babylon,
They shake at revived whole wide world Empire of Rome.

Ultimate Hero

He's the innocent, spotless Lamb,
Son of God who's called 'I Am',
How He suffered for the lost,
He left behind an empty cross.
After three days, an empty tomb,
Here where death could find no room,
He takes these keys of death and Hell,
Makes Satan's kingdom quake and quell,
Set Noah's family free from prison,
All because He died and has risen.
He provides the sinner's pardon,
Meets young Mary in a garden,
Serves apostles fish on a shore,
Gives them life for evermore.
He ascends to Heaven above,
Joins his father in perfect love.
Then He sends His tongues of fire,
Fills Christian hearts with desire.
Jesus on clouds, His trumpet sounds,
All Christians rise up from the ground,
To meet their Saviour in the air,
With his army of angels gathered there,
This time He comes, bold as a Lion,
On his mission to conquer Zion.
Out of his mouth comes a sharpened sword,
This King of Kings and Lord of Lords.
He's riding on his great white horse,
Takes this wicked world by force,

Where He engages in spiritual warfare,
With the princes and powers of the air,
His angel binds Satan in their midst,
And sends him hurtling down in the abyss.
Just before his millennial reign,
Jesus Christ will come again,
He'll stand feet apart on Mount of Olives,
Below will flow fresh mighty rivers,
Down through the great Rift Valley,
That brings life to the once Dead Sea.
A temple on mountain of the Lord,
The saved all worship in one accord,
At the end of a thousand years,
Satan's released and reappears,
Defeated cast in the lake of fire,
His followers scream in a place so dire,
Dead come before the great white throne,
And all these wicked He'll disown.
He'll create a new heaven and earth,
A new Jerusalem filled with mirth.

Forever England

We're under a swinging sign in a Cotswold village,
A Tudor Inn that's called the Jenny Wren,
We carry on through a gate and over a bridge,
Find ourselves at home in an English garden.
We're caught up in the flower bed's deep fragrance,
The rhododendrons red as a maiden's blush,
Overcome by the garden's beautiful presence,
Cheered by those whistling notes from a song thrush,
We come across the quaintest of wishing wells;
Overlooking white lilies in a pond,
Further on a carpet of swaying bluebells,
Enhance that soaring fountain just beyond.
We hear sparrows chat under the cottage eaves,
A farrier rides by on his horse and cart,
Live in a time when our soul no longer grieves,
Plucking those musical strings within our heart,
We sniff those hanging purple lanterns of lilac,
Amble down an English country lane,
Counting those chimes from that old church clock,
Then we hear the cuckoo calling again.
After we've climbed over a wooden stile,
Buttercup globes light up those meadows green,
That moment when we feel the spring sun smile;
See how it sparkles on a serpentine stream,
Hear a woodpecker tapping on bark,
When we pass through creaking kissing gates,
Lifted up watching a rising trilling lark,
We come to where our demon lover waits.

Wherever we walk we hear this haunting song,
That moves every patriotic man,
We nurse in our breast our beloved Albion
And we realise there'll always be an England.

Soul Power

Solar and lunar rays fuel my soul power,
Among the millions of stars that seem to devour,
On the clouds of idolatry, I ride
My dark horse in a long black cloak of pride,
All my energy has fallen under its spell,
Feeling the fury from the flames in Hell,
Meeting with the princes and powers of the air,
See that serpent, the dragon leaving his lair,
Haunting, hovering over many regions,
Leading his army of demonic legions,
Masquerading above a sleepy town,
Then like a thunder bolt booming around,
Flashing through corridors and halls of night,
I watch this dragon change to an angel of light.

Death Valley

Warrior horse riders come through a mirage,
Suddenly break into a warlike charge,
Their horse hoofs beating on desert sand,
Will leave a trail of blood through every land,
They follow a vulture flying overhead,
As they ride through a dried-up riverbed,
Underneath a scorching bright sun at noon,
Galloping through a valley of death with a boom;
Knowing that a darker day will not dawn,
Seeing a genie's face inside a dusty storm,
Their horses snort brimstone into a gorge,
Beneath the skies red as a fiery forge,
A star and crescent moon for all to see,
They dart quick as lightning through Death Valley.

Grim Reaper

I'm the Grim Reaper in drooping black hood,
Breathe an ill wind that's blowing no good,
Sweeping my scythe hither and thither,
All there before me will wilt and whither.
I've journeyed so far from the land of the dead,
Embracing the darkness and lantern led,
The bigger the harvest the greater my power,
All on my path, I'll seek to devour.
During a plague, I'll knock on your door,
Sparing neither the rich nor the poor,
Passing the people that starve at their gate,
I wallow in woe and I'm filled with hate.
Hark the church bell, so let it knell,
Set off my howling black hounds in Hell,
Enjoy my despair with no sense of hope,
Bodies that swing from a hangman's rope,
Cheer with those gathered around the guillotine,
Sound of the cutter, a terrifying scream,
The fiercer the fighting, the greater my yield,
With the dead piled up on a battlefield,
Fate's the same for a coward or the brave,
My appetite's greedier than the grave.

Rievaulx Abbey

Cistercian Monks all chant from Rievaulx Abbey,
Surrounded by white sheep on sunny hills,
Peasants work in the peaceful Rye Valley,
Listening to this heavenly music that fills
The abbey and brings alive its architecture,
Through time, on a mystical sea of song,
Where early English arches rise in grandeur,
That revives a lost age, long gone.
Shafts of light shine through the stained-glass windows,
And the Holy Spirit's wings of calm
Inspires a holiness that moves and flows,
Enhanced by words spoken from ninety-first psalm,
Monks fall prostrate before the sacred altar,
When their cycle reaches its climax at prime,
And that red sun now rises from its bed,
That time when their worship touches the sublime.

Monks assemble together singing vespers,
Near candles on either side of cross aflame,
They feel the harmonies flowing down from Heaven,
Showers of blessing falling like fresh rain.
They're awakened by dark psychic power,
Find they're being put through their paces,
Facing some demons that threaten to devour,
Staring from the ceiling with glowing faces,
And a bitter, black-tongued giggling gargoyle,
Red imps spring up and are jumping around,
Out of that fire and fury up from Hell,

All trespassing on this hallowed ground;
The brothers engage in spiritual warfare,
Rebuke the Devil standing at the door,
Amazed how quickly his evil spirits disperse,
Right out of the abbey with a roar.

They're singing on their way to midnight mass,
Darkness, thicker than black heart of the woods,
They hold up candlelit lanterns, hanging from poles,
Robed in dazzling white cloaks and pointed hoods,
Walk in procession over the fleur-de-lis tiles,
No sooner when they stand behind the stalls,
Watching Heaven come down from golden heights,
Abbey's arches shine like Heaven's halls,
Where seraphs are burning in holy fire,
Swinging their smoking bowls of sweet incense,
They hear some melodies sound from an angel's lyre,
All overwhelmed by the Lord Almighty's presence;
Seeing floating specks of golden dust,
Glittering and all glowing in God's glory,
Monks are radiating in this brilliant light,
Here at Rievaulx Abbey in Rye Valley.

Monastery Garden

Here in the heart of a monastery garden,
I feel the Almighty's presence in the morn,
Breathing down from his holy mountain,
I court His freshness like the first new dawn.
In that moment when dews of day descend,
Hear the nuns' angelic voices at prime,
Making all my body hair stand on end,
Now every bird's note comes in on time.

When I hear the nuns' plainchant at sext,
I remember when the garden smiled,
Wonder what would ever happen next,
Catching a vision with the eyes of a child,
Busy counting those ripples in a stream,
Like violin strings vibrating in sound,
Drawing me deeper into its mystical theme,
Seems I'm standing on holy ground.
I'm so uplifted by a cuckoo calling,
Bees all humming in the honeysuckle,
In the distance waterfalls are roaring,
Nearby where the rocky rivers chuckle;
Under Heaven's glory that fills the skies,
I see the flowers all glowing in harmony,
Overwhelmed by soaring butterflies,
I find this simplicity thrills me.

The nuns are singing 'Kyrie eleison',
Mood at vespers makes me more intense,

I hear the warm earth breaking out in song,
Sniff the flowers deep fragrance like incense
Rising, carried on a gentle breeze,
Under darkening skies all red and mauve,
I'm enraptured with ritual rooks in the trees,
Stirring up that ancient tuneful grove,
When I look deep down into the vale,
Pure white lambs graze on a dark green hill,
I'm enchanted by a nightingale,
The rhythm from a grinding watermill,
I watch a rag and bone man click his heels,
Leading his shire horse over a bridge,
And his jolting cart with clattering wheels,
There on his way from the sleepy sunset village.

I rise up from my bed in the dead of night,
Rush to hear the nuns all singing at nocturnes,
Monastery windows are flickering in candlelight,
And fireflies sparkling under Grecian urns,
It seems I'm standing with the world at my feet;
Staring into that moonlit lily pond,
My spirit feeling at one with the cosmic beat,
With the glorious stars all shining beyond,
Then I make my way to bubbling springs,
With a sense of eternity reigning in my being
And hear the brushing from angels' wings,
Know the heavenly realms and meet my King,
Here my first love comes to remembrance,
When I became the most contented of men,
Find myself blessed with perfect innocence,
Here in the heart of this monastery garden.

The Lord's Pilgrimage in England

Lord God walks through the English Mountains,
Dazzling white train fills the valleys,
Majesty from the one, who reigns,
Shines like fire through forest trees.

Stately presence like a golden lion,
Ancient feet of burnished bronze,
On His pilgrimage from Zion,
And He fills his Church with songs.

He mounts up like an eagle on high,
Soaring above a cherubim's wings,
Where His glory fills the skies,
This mighty awesome King of Kings.

See how His purity shines above,
Power that glows in His lightning strikes,
Seraphim show His mercy and love,
Praise to the holiest in the heights.

Lamb of God on throne of thrones,
Gazes on a sapphire sea,
Glitters brighter than precious stones,
Here in the depths of eternity.

How his Spirit trails through England,
Lighting streets in every city,
Almighty, with uplifted hand,

Now pardons and sets its captives free.

Heavenly Father's perfect presence,
Shines in a circle of emerald green,
Portrays a picture of pure innocence,
There in those English pastures seen.

Then He travels from north to south,
Moving on from east to west,
Brings new life by word of mouth,
Offers comfort, peace and rest.

Supreme Being then appears,
At those Christian sacred sites,
Places soaked in prayer for years,
Now shine in everlasting light.

High on Glastonbury's Tor,
Comes to an ageless church tower,
One who lives for evermore
And He shines in light and power.

All around Him seems so still,
Treading along a pilgrim's path,
Stops a moment at Wearyall Hill,
Right near Joseph's budding staff.

There He stands in the abbey's ruins,
And remembers every prayer,
Hears the monks chant their anthems,
Rise like incense in the air.

Memories of ancient lake in mind,
Looking at the isle of Avalon,
Casts his thoughts way back in time,
Arthurian legend will go on.

Later He visits the historic town,
Wanders through its thriving market,
Transforms the villages all around,
Set in the heart of Somerset.

Here He shines his light divine,
On his Holy Grail of suffering,
Overflows red with wine,
There from an ever-bubbling spring.

Light in Dark December

How we long for light in dark December,
When our cheeks and fingertips are cold,
Retrace our footsteps, reflect and remember,
See the sunshine on willows like burnished gold.
We gaze at the quilted patchwork evening skies,
Display their colours of red, yellow and mauve,
And right in the heart of an ancient oak tree lies
That moonlit mistletoe in Druid's Drove.
We shudder at icicles on a shepherd's hut,
Watch him driving his flock of sheep downhill,
And pass ice skaters eating roasted chestnuts,
A warm stove brings us relief from winter's chill.
Now the skies turn to a deeper purple,
We walk down country lanes with their frosted hedges,
High in some vicarage trees, rooks caw and circle,
Below we see children riding on their sledges.
Later we come across a stately home,
Its architecture seems like frozen music,
Playing a symphony, all in perfect tone,
With its melody moving our inner spirit.
It continues the theme in a classical-styled garden,
Exploring our finest feelings with its symmetry,
And rising to a climax like a fountain,
Resound the glory from the eighteenth century.
We follow the shepherd down to his village,
Laugh at a maiden swearing over her clothes,
Hanging stiff as starch on her washing line,
We turn, catch a glimpse from a parson's red nose

As he dances to the merry church bells that chime,
Hear him tap on a water butt that's frozen hard,
We see some choirboys walking down a path,
Between the glistening graves in a churchyard.
We freeze at a ghost's appearance on holy ground,
But moved voices singing a Bach chorale,
Followed by an organ's majestic sound,
Then hear a rendering of 'The First Nowell.'
We join with yokels inside the Queen of Hearts,
And watch the traditional burning Yuletide log,
Sizzling, crackling, sometimes spitting sparks,
Enjoy a feast from the farmer's roasted hog.
There in a corner we hear the parson snore,
A busty barmaid serves us tankards of beer,
Hear carol singers, and who stands at the door?
And keeps on knocking, year after year?

King of Kings

Star shines over Bethlehem,
Christ Child lies asleep on hay,
The apple of his Father's eye,
One day, be the light and way.
Shepherds abiding in the fields,
Watching over their flocks by night,
Glory of the Lord reveals
That power in His angels bright.

Shepherds gather to see the boy,
Resting in a stinky stable,
All their hearts are filled with joy,
Their Saviour in a makeshift cradle,
Three wise men come from the east,
Bearing all their precious gifts,
Gazing on the Prince of Peace,
And the Holy Spirit uplifts.

Myrrh predicts His painful death,
Hanging down on wooden cross,
Last words from His dying breath,
Heartfelt cries for the lost.
Crown of thorns pressed in his head,
He's the creator of all things,
Third day rises from the dead,
Now He's Lord and King of Kings.

Printed in Great Britain
by Amazon